A GOOD FIT
FOR ALL KIDS

A GOOD FIT FOR ALL KIDS

Collaborating to Teach Writing in Diverse, Inclusive Settings

KELLY CHANDLER-OLCOTT

HARVARD EDUCATION PRESS
CAMBRIDGE, MASSACHUSETTS

Paperback ISBN 978-1-68253-343-7
Library Edition ISBN 978-1-68253-344-4

CIP data is on file with the Library of Congress.

Published by Harvard Education Press,
an imprint of the Harvard Education Publishing Group

Harvard Education Press
8 Story Street
Cambridge, MA 02138

Cover Design: Ciano Design
Cover Photo: Marc Volk/Getty Images

The typefaces used in this book are Palatino LT Std and Myriad Pro

For Jodi and John, there from the start

Contents

Introduction

I t's the last Friday morning in July, and a crowd has gathered for the Robinson Summer Writing Institute's end-of-program celebration. Nearly all of the forty-five students who have completed the three-week program will enroll as ninth graders at Robinson High School in the fall.[1] They occupy the first few rows of the darkened large-group instruction room, known as the LGIR, with their guests seated behind them and their summer teachers standing in the aisles.

On a screen at the front of the room, a presentation begins. Constructed using the free software Microsoft Photo Story 3, it features two slides about each participant. The first slide includes the student's name and photograph; the next slide has the title and a sentence or two from a personal narrative students composed during the program. Soft piano music plays under each student's audiotaped narration of the text, with accents hinting at a wide range of first languages, including Arabic, Kiswahili, and Somali. The audience pays close attention, chuckling and sighing at content like the following:

"Almost Lost It": It was the worst pain I ever felt in my life. It felt like the world's tallest man pulling on it. (Bashiir)

"Flying Colors": I knew he would be mobbed; it's just the way my friends are. They tend to swarm people. (Bethany)

"My First Day of School": I came to the United States and was 16 when I first learned to read. (Ibrahim)

"Lockdown": I guess you live and you learn . . . right? (Kiara)

"One Week, Two Graduates": I could feel the success flowing through the air. I think I inhaled it. (Etan)

Both the titles and the excerpts reveal that students have explored varied topics from their lives, including athletic triumphs and defeats, academic challenges, family trips and migrations, noteworthy performances, accidents and injuries, and adventures with pets. A slide at the end of the presentation invites attendees to browse a complete collection of printed narratives displayed on a table just outside the auditorium. (Student participants will receive a cleanly edited version of their essay to take home in a folder that also includes a certificate, summer reading recommendations, and the URL address for the program's YouTube channel.)

When the last strains of music fade away, the lights return. Pairs of teachers lead guests to the library and two adjoining computer labs for the celebration's next component, during which small groups of students will screen two-to-four-minute movies—digital stories in the parlance of the program—they created with Photo Story 3. Each group identified a topic of interest related to the program's two essential questions (EQs): *Why write?* and *How does writing affect me and the world?* They worked together to conduct internet research and, in some cases, first-person interviews to investigate their topics; author a script for their audiotaped narration; and combine that narration with carefully selected images and music. Now, before their work is seen by an audience for the first time, they introduce themselves and prepare to field questions.

Although the digital stories vary in length and quality, every single one presents new information, addresses an EQ, and harnesses the multimedia capability of the software. Every single group draws on meaningful contributions from each member. And nearly every single kid smiles publicly—some broadly, some a little more subtly—at the warm applause their compositions receive from attendees.

Big Ideas of This Book

For four years, between 2010 and 2013, I was fortunate to serve as the director of the Robinson Summer Writing Institute, working side by side with a committed staff of teachers from Brown Central Schools, a midsize urban district, in an initiative intended to promote writing achievement and engagement for students like Bashiir, Bethany, Ibrahim, Kiara, and Etan. I open this book with scenes from the institute's fourth annual end-of-program celebration, because they exemplify some big ideas of the program and of this book, which seeks to highlight the power of collaborative approaches for teaching writing to youth in diverse, inclusive classrooms. I hope that the story of the Robinson institute will support secondary teachers and school leaders in working together to construct writing pedagogy that responds to all adolescents' strengths, needs, and interests.

First and foremost, the institute was designed as a learning community that balanced the individual with the collective. The presentation of snippets from each student's personal narrative honored their distinct appearances, voices, histories, interests, and skill levels as writers. The instruction preceding the celebration was grounded in our team's commitment to knowing kids well and using that knowledge. Bashiir, a Somali immigrant with interrupted education, needed supports and challenges that were different from those of Bethany, a native speaker of English who had experienced continuous schooling in the United States. Those differences, however, were framed as resources to be leveraged, not deficits to be managed. Bethany and Bashiir explored the same rigorous curriculum and composed their writing in the same focal genres. Each was viewed as having things to learn and things to teach one another. Groupings and opportunities for interaction were designed to maximize heterogeneity and inclusion, not to create levels or tracks in the name of remediation or acceleration. One of my contentions in this book, in fact, is that diverse, inclusive classrooms typically represent the best contexts for all learners to develop writing proficiency, regardless of the labels affixed on them by schools.[2]

The writing institute also foregrounded teacher learning in community. Although the celebration spotlighted student work, it included a moment when the institute staff was recognized as well. That this introduction took place in pairs was no accident, as the work of the previous three weeks (and indeed several months before that) had been relentlessly collaborative, with teachers spending as much time on planning and examining student work as they had interacting with youth. This aspect of the program was discussed only briefly with students and their guests, but it was key to the program's vision from its launch.

Another central argument of this book, then, is that the success that writers with diverse profiles found within the institute depended not just on their collaboration with peers but also on collaboration by adults. Each three-hour instructional block with learners was sandwiched between precise, purposeful planning and debriefing sessions by the full institute team and opportunities for pairs of teachers working closely together to calibrate expectations and coordinate their approaches. Janice, a Robinson teacher of English and special education and an institute staff member in Years 1–4, explained the relationship between inclusive student success and the unusual degree of teacher collaboration this way:

> I thought that the opportunity to collaborate with a group of professionals . . . that have actually had different training and different experiences and come from different places was really powerful. All those voices and all of those thoughts on the table together helped us craft something that was *a good fit for all kids*, not just a specific kind of kid that aligns with a specific type of teacher.

This same idea rippled through interviews with nearly every staff member who worked in the program—a degree of consensus that led me to borrow Janice's language for the title of this book.

The closing celebration reflects another aspect of the institute that might have been difficult for guests to notice: its status as a space for design-based research. More specifically, my collaborators and I conceptualized the institute from the beginning as a formative experiment, an approach intended to "bring about positive change in education environments through creative, innovative, instructional interventions grounded in theory and guided by systematic data collection and analysis."[3] As such, many features of the celebration—and the program more broadly—remained consistent over four years, including exploration of both print and digital genres and co-planning and co-teaching by the staff. These features represented what design researchers call essential elements, components of an intervention that are built into the original framework such that changing them would undermine its integrity.[4]

Other aspects of the celebration and the larger program, however, were deliberately adjusted to enhance the experience and improve learning for both youth and adults. For instance, our team's approach to showcasing students' personal narratives during the celebration changed significantly from Year 1, when teachers selected a trio of students, all of them native English speakers, to read exemplary texts aloud to the audience, to Year 4, when every member of the multicultural and multilingual cohort was featured. Such adjustments were grounded in careful analysis of varied data sources at multiple intervals: daily, during afternoon planning; annually, between program iterations; and longitudinally, across iterations. The dynamic program yielded by this process over time was far stronger and more inclusive than the original blueprint delivered with static consistency could have been. Although this is a book intended primarily for practitioners, not researchers, another of my contentions is that practitioner involvement in collaborative research creates better research and better practitioners.

What We Know About Writing, Equity, and Inclusion

Indeed, extant research suggests some sobering historical trends related to writing instruction and achievement for diverse groups of adolescents. Despite the increasing presence of writing in various print and digital forms for many people in contemporary society, writing has been a neglected curricular area in the United States for many years. Legislation such as the 2001 No Child Left Behind Act focused disproportionate attention, resources, and accountability pressures on reading rather than writing. Most secondary teachers receive little formal training to teach writing during their preparation programs, and few experience sustained on-the-job support in this area unless they are lucky enough to have access to an established professional network such as a National Writing Project site.

Perhaps not surprisingly, these trends coincide with writing achievement patterns that leave much to be desired. According to the most recent national achievement snapshot, just 27 percent of eighth graders and 27 percent of eleventh graders scored at or above the "Proficient" level in writing.[5] Even more concerning, the overall scores mask significant achievement gaps for numerous groups that have been traditionally underserved in school, such as English learners, students with disabilities, and students of color. Although these gaps are complicated, reflecting a host of beyond-school factors, including poverty, structural racism, and the politicization of learning standards and tests, differences in instructional practices contribute as well.[6] Both English learners and students with disabilities, for example, have been shown to write less in school and to receive less feedback from their teachers, while low-income students use technology more often for drills and intervention and less often for authentic reading and writing purposes than their more advantaged peers.[7]

These concerning trends may be interrupted, however, by some promising recent developments. The adoption of the Common Core English Language Arts and Literacy Standards in most states, while not without controversy, has elevated writing, both in English and in other subject areas, from the poor stepchild of reading to an important area of focus in its own right. Documentation of the greater writing demands in many careers and decreased tolerance for disparate outcomes as revealed by data disaggregation have created new urgency to teach all students to write well, not just a select few. And the explosion of interest in structures to develop in-service educators' expertise, including professional learning communities and Japanese-inspired lesson study, hints at new willingness to rethink and revise current ways of doing business in schools.[8]

A growing body of literature points the way to possibility when teachers resist deficit orientations to name, sustain, and extend student writers' varied resources for learning.[9] For example, when individuals with autism who struggle with unreliable oral communication learn to type, they access the general education curriculum and advocate for change in schools and beyond. When low-income African American youth confronted with the gentrification of their neighborhood use participatory action research tools, they become powerful communicators in both print and digital genres. When resettled refugees learning English join online communities, they retain connections to their cultural heritage and identity while developing academic language and literacy. Common enabling factors emerge across the examples, including presumption of student competence, varied purposes for writing, explicit instruction around needed strategies, ample time for composing, and social interaction with peers and teachers.[10] When these conditions are met, writing achievement gaps begin to seem a lot less inevitable for groups that were predictably disadvantaged in the past.

Who I Am and Why I Wrote This Book

I am a former high school English and social studies teacher who now works as a university-based teacher educator. My focus is on preparing teachers who see it as a crucial part of their jobs to help middle and high school students use literacy to learn and communicate in powerful, discipline-specific ways.

I have long believed summer to be an important resource for learning, with some of my most transformational experiences as an educator taking place during that time of year. In my first paid job in education, at the age of nineteen, I served as a counselor and literacy instructor in a residential summer enrichment program for teens sponsored by the Maine Aspirations Compact. For three years during my secondary teaching career, I directed a summer book club for youth that combined informal discussion of contemporary literature with hiking, playing board games, going to the beach, and other activities. When I moved into higher education, I designed several short-term electives for graduate students that took advantage of summer factors such as reduced curricular constraints and the focus associated with a compressed format. Experiences like these convinced me of the potential for risk taking, skill development, relationship building, and renewal that summer initiatives can present to both teachers and learners.

Another key component of my background is that I have worked for the past twenty years in the Syracuse University School of Education, an institution with a deep, abiding commitment to diversity and inclusion. My literacy classes routinely include students with general education majors such as mathematics and music alongside those studying to be special educators—a mix that enriches everyone. My colleagues, past and present, have contributed to cutting-edge research and advocacy intended to create equitable, vibrant, and welcoming learning communities for all. I have sought to link the institute directly with those traditions.

Last but not least, I have a long history of designing and researching literacy instruction of varying kinds in partnership with K–12 professionals. A number of these projects have been situated in the Brown district, including a one-to-one literacy tutoring program delivered by college students; an investigation of the literacy demands of new, standards-based mathematics curricula for middle and high school; and an inclusive, integrated humanities program delivered by teachers of English, social studies, and special education.[11]

The Robinson writing institute sits at the intersection of these patterns in my professional history. I used insights from each of these experiences to design, direct, and disseminate insights from the program, which was annually the highlight of my academic calendar. Over the years, I have written about numerous program components, including grouping strategies, the nonfiction focus of our writer's notebooks, and how our approaches to co-teaching supported differentiation for varied learning needs.[12] These publications offered a vantage point on what was valuable about the work, but none captured the components' interplay. Consequently, I wrote this book both for myself, to understand how those components fit together and amplified each other, and for others, to contribute to an ongoing conversation about how to enact an ambitious vision of writing pedagogy in diverse, inclusive settings.

The book is single-authored in the narrowest, most traditional sense of that word. I am the one who sat inside on too many sunny days to generate these particular words, and I am the one responsible for whether they are the right words. But you'll notice as you move through these pages that I use first-person plural ("we," "us," and "our") far more often than I use first-person singular ("I," "me," and "my") to describe the work. This deliberate linguistic choice is intended to represent the joint construction of nearly every good idea you'll find here. As I'll elucidate further in subsequent chapters, what the institute accomplished was always a function of its collaborative design, delivery, and refinement.

How the Robinson Story Might Help You

In addition to the writing I mentioned above, I have made many face-to-face presentations about the institute in classes, at conferences, and during professional development workshops. It's not unusual for these audiences to find the Robinson story fascinating at first but to then begin poking holes in the recommendations I make based on a perceived lack of alignment between the institute context and what many call "the real world" of K–12 schooling. I understand these impulses and acknowledge how institute features such as low teacher-student ratios, the absence of grading requirements, and curricular flexibility have contributed to learning outcomes that are more difficult to achieve in typical schools with more limited resources and competing concerns.

But I've also seen, again and again, that the more people learn about the project, and the more opportunities they have to consider implications for their own professional lives, the easier it becomes for them to imagine changes in their own varied contexts that are informed and inspired by what my Robinson colleagues and students were able to accomplish in a particular space, at a particular time, under particular conditions. From these interactions, I envision three main audiences for this book, each with distinct and overlapping interests.

If you are a school or central office administrator, this book will help you think about structures you could put in place to build capacity for high-quality writing instruction, particularly for students who have traditionally been underserved in school. It will demonstrate the desirability of seeding, supporting, and studying learning communities among your own personnel rather than purchasing and monitoring the implementation of writing-focused programs designed by others.

If you are an instructional coach or department leader, the book will offer descriptions of facilitation roles you may play and tools you may offer to promote teacher learning with respect to improving writing instruction for all students. It will help you not only to advocate for structural change and needed resources with building and district administrators but also to demonstrate instructional practices you can recommend (or implement collaboratively) with the colleagues you support.

If you are (or will soon be) a classroom teacher, the book will help you adopt, adapt, or refine instructional practices such as fostering inquiry, modeling, and conferring that are proven to support writing success for students with widely varying needs. It will demonstrate ways to collaborate with other adults that will amplify your impact and, perhaps, ease the burdens associated with navigating new mandates and increased expectations on your own. And it will help you make a case to decision-makers in your context for needed time, space, and resources.

With all three constituencies, I hope the book will offer promising possibilities and challenge deficit perspectives about culturally and linguistically diverse students and the adults who teach them. I hope it will demonstrate the value of inclusive settings for such work rather than learning environments tracked and leveled based on perceived ability, language, and disability status. And I hope it will illustrate that creating classroom spaces that are a "good fit for all" is inextricably linked to how we see each other as resources—both adults and students—and how we work together to achieve common goals.

How This Book Is Organized

In addition to this introduction, the book has eight chapters. All eight begin with a narrative vignette in present tense intended to immerse you as the reader in different aspects of the institute as richly and concretely as possible. Some of these vignettes depict whole-program or small-group instruction when students were present, while others portray collaborative sessions during which staff members planned instruction and analyzed student work. My highlighting of both types of interaction in the openings is meant to signal their equivalent importance in my mind to the success of the project. To emphasize the longitudinal nature of this work, I also chose vignettes from across the four-year time frame.

Chapter 1 provides an overview of the Robinson context, including an account of the early college partnership in which the writing institute was embedded. It introduces both the teachers and the students who participated in the institute, and it describes the various components of the program. It concludes with discussion of the data sources our team drew on for both program improvement and research findings and makes some preliminary assertions, to be supported more fully in subsequent chapters, about how my collaborators and I judged its success.

The next six chapters represent the instructional heart of the book, and as such, they are presented with parallel structure. Each is divided into two or three main sections illustrated by numerous samples and examples of student work, selected with care to illustrate participant diversity in terms of gender, race/ethnicity, language, disability status, year of attendance, and other factors. Each concludes with a Tips and Takeaways section, in bulleted form, that lists recommendations about how you might implement ideas from the chapter in a school setting and, where relevant, whom you might recruit as allies or collaborators. All six of these chapters are explicit about (1) how my collaborators and I adjusted our approaches as a result of our ongoing design-based research and (2) how we leveraged the affordances of co-planning and co-teaching within a professional learning community to better address students' varied needs.

In terms of content, chapter 2 focuses on collaborative tools and processes we used as staff to design and refine the instruction described in other portions of the book. Chapter 3 addresses our inquiry stance toward writing, with sections on the role of essential questions in the program, particularly with digital stories, and on the "noticings" routine we employed with varied exemplar texts, including those authored by previous youth participants. Chapter 4 describes our use of the writer's notebook as a multifaceted tool to promote writing development in general as well as to support students' production of and reflection on the focal genres. Chapter 5 takes up the topics of modeling and mentoring, with particular emphasis on teachers' process-related "think-alouds" and on invited presentations by a diverse slate of guest writers from the community about how they use writing in their personal and professional lives. Chapter 6 presents conferences as a key site for enacting our "strengths-first" perspective while offering differentiated support to individuals. Serving as a sort of bookend, chapter 7 revisits the collaboration theme of chapter 2 but this time with a focus on supporting writing-related interactions among students, not just the staff.

At the end of the book, in chapter 8, I discuss themes about curriculum, collaboration, and community that cut across the four iterations of the institute and the accompanying research. Next I describe several initiatives that staff members or I pursued beyond the program that had roots in our shared work within the institute. I conclude with a series of suggestions about how you might apply what you've learned from the book to collaborative contexts beyond the individual classroom that matter to you. These suggestions are intended to provide a wider view on institute-inspired change than the more instructionally focused tips and takeaways from previous chapters.

CHAPTER 1

The Robinson Summer Writing Institute

It's Wednesday, Day 3 of our fourth consecutive year of running the Robinson Summer Writing Institute. Teachers and students are returning to the LGIR from classrooms where they have been discussing an exemplar text and generating possible topics for their personal narratives. Instructions for participating in closing meeting, scheduled for the final twenty minutes of today's instructional session, are summarized on a PowerPoint slide with these bullets:

- Write for five uninterrupted minutes about why you decorated your writer's notebook cover the way you did: explain the choices you made and what they show about you as a person.
- Count your words and write the number down at the end of your entry.
- Be BRAVE: volunteer to share your cover and your writing at the projector.

When all three teaching teams have arrived and everyone has settled into seats, students begin to tackle the prompt.

As I am circulating to observe kids at work, Winton, a native English-speaking African American boy, gets my attention and asks if he can share—a clear indication that he has read all the way to the third bullet. When Jake, who is co-facilitating the meeting, calls time and asks who wants to share, I point to Winton, and Jake selects him, along with three other volunteers. All four share their notebook covers under the document camera and explain the significance of their image selections, with some summarizing their entries orally and others reading bits from their notebooks verbatim. Winton highlights a photograph of rapper and poet Tupac Shakur on his cover, explaining, "He lived a life we can't imagine."

When the sharing is finished, I join Jake at the front of the room and remind students about my earlier promise to teach them some different ways to appreciate community members for their contributions. I ask them to give two snaps, the appreciation they learned on Day 1, to the four volunteers who just shared their writing; then I put both of my hands in the air and waggle my fingers silently to model another option for demonstrating approbation. "Writing fingers?" Winton asks loudly and mimes furious typing, which makes everyone, both adolescents and adults, laugh. I say no, that the gesture represents a form of applause in the Deaf community, but that I think I might like his articulation better given our writing focus. And, indeed, Winton's phrase will stick: for the remainder of the program, students being recognized for accomplishments of one kind or another will call for "writing fingers" just as readily as they choose traditional claps, snaps, or stomps.

This chapter provides an overview of the summer writing institute at the center of this book. I open with this scene because it represents some key ideas at the heart of the program, including our use of varied spaces, tools, and teaching configurations during instruction as well as our commitment to building a supportive, playful, and invitational culture for students to link their experiences to their writing. In the first section I offer some history and background for the institute, describing the school context and explaining how the project was situated within a broader school-university partnership. Next I describe the program itself, introducing the staff and student participants and presenting key program components. In the final section I discuss the information sources my collaborators and I used to draw conclusions about the program's effectiveness and to make ongoing adjustments for its improvement.

History and Background of the Institute

Teachers and leaders at Robinson High School, where the institute was located, were aware that some of the most troubling trends when it came to writing achievement were relevant for portions of their student body. Robinson staff and families saw the ethnic and racial diversity of its approximately thirteen hundred students (60 percent Black or African American, 22 percent White, 10 percent Asian or Pacific Islander, and

7 percent Hispanic or Latino when the program began) as a strength, as do I. But the reporting categories for demographic data obscured a notable increase in the number of refugee students from African and Asian countries. (Students from Somalia or Sudan, for example, were classified with the same Black/African American label as native-born Black students, despite differences in their English proficiency and access to formal schooling.) Nearly two-thirds of Robinson students were eligible for free or reduced-price lunch. Perhaps not surprising, given the high correlations between both socioeconomic status and English proficiency and standardized test scores, Robinson's passing percentages on the state English language arts test were in the mid-fifties across a span of several years. (The pass rate was even lower for students with disabilities, who represented about 15 percent of the student body.) Such score patterns subjected the school to state surveillance and, eventually, some mandated restructuring. Some Robinson students were clearly thriving, particularly those in advanced courses, and no one in the building viewed the state test scores as the final word on student achievement. But acknowledgment was growing that the staff could, and should, work with community stakeholders to address disparate outcomes for particular student groups.

In 2009, as one prong of such an effort, Brown district leaders undertook a partnership with my university to transform Robinson into an early college high school, where students could earn up to two years of college credit before graduation. The early college premise is that acceleration with support, not remediation, creates motivation for youth to excel, including those from groups underrepresented in college.[1] In addition to the dual-enrollment programs characteristic of all early colleges, the partnership sponsored campus visits, after-school tutoring, and Saturday enrichment workshops.

I was invited to join the early college initiative when the partnership's leaders identified writing, one of my scholarly interests, as a focus due to its influence on postsecondary success. At the time, I had a nearly decade-long relationship with Robinson mostly focused on student-teaching placements and alumni hiring from the English Education program I coordinated. My research and professional development efforts were situated at Brown but at the middle level, where I had most recently worked with a colleague, Kathleen Hinchman, and a trio of teachers to co-design and study an inclusive, integrated humanities class. This work helped establish my credibility with the Robinson staff and gave me a good sense of the curriculum and instruction to which Robinson students had likely been exposed in the feeder schools they attended. I was excited by the early college partnership's invitation.

Given a belief within the partnership that Robinson's eleven English teachers would be central to any writing-focused reform within the school, my work began with them. During two focus groups, they spoke candidly and reflectively with me and one another about concerns that writing instruction in the school did not adequately serve English learners or African Americans. Their desire to address these patterns led us to launch a voluntary book club focused on teaching writing to diverse populations. Early college grant monies covered the costs of purchasing professional texts on this topic for anyone who wanted to participate.[2] Six English teachers explored these texts with me and Bryan Crandall, a PhD advisee of mine with deep ties to the National Writing Project, during three ninety-minute discussions that summer. Sharing our ideas over takeout Chinese food in the Robinson library began to build the trust and mutual understanding needed to launch the institute the following summer.

First, however, the department and I embarked on a yearlong series of professional development (PD) sessions intended to support implementation of insights from our summer reading as well as other approaches to teaching writing aligned with teachers' goals. The sessions took place monthly during the school day, to lessen the burden on busy teachers. Each session lasted about two and a half hours and was scheduled once in the morning, once in the afternoon, allowing teachers to share substitutes.

My selection of content was informed by a guidance document I drafted and shared with teachers and partnership leaders. My recommendations, reproduced in figure 1.1, drew on my knowledge of the scholarly and practical literature on teaching writing along with my knowledge of the Robinson context to that point. I focused on high-utility approaches such as teacher think-alouds, study of mentor texts, and one-to-one conferences that I conjectured would make writing strategies and genre demands more explicit to diverse populations. A typical PD session included modeling of an approach such as a think-aloud, discussion of how the approach might be embedded in a typical Robinson unit given district directives and building preferences, and debriefing of teachers' experiences in their classrooms during the preceding month.

FIGURE 1.1   Guidance document for academic-year professional development

Ideas for Improving Writing Instruction at Robinson

Increase volume of writing for ALL students

- Distinguish between informal and formal writing and note opportunities for both in teacher plans.
- Link writing-to-learn opportunities more explicitly to public genres.
- Develop a tracking system beyond teacher plans to ensure that some groups (e.g., ELLs, students with disabilities) do not write less than peers because of diminished expectations/opportunity.
- Provide opportunities for student choice, including with writer's notebooks.
- Pair English teachers deliberately with teachers from other departments to support writing-to-learn across the curriculum.

Vary genres to which students will be exposed

- Use district portfolio expectations as starting point for genre selection.
- Analyze the various demands of those pieces.
- Link reading and writing more closely, reducing emphasis on writing about novels.
- Place more emphasis on digital genres.

Provide high-quality models of writing tasks

- Develop a shared protocol for teacher think-alouds.
- Develop a shared protocol to analyze various kinds of published writing for structure and craft.
- Share high-quality peer models in process.
- Collect high-quality peer models for use with future classes.

Conduct planful (not just spontaneous) writing conferences

- Develop common expectations for how to prepare for 1–1 and small-group conferences.
- Develop whole-class management strategies that promote independence.
- Develop shared expectations for how to use additional support personnel (e.g., push-in teachers in inclusive classrooms) effectively.

Increase meaningful social interaction around writing

- Provide authentic audiences for finished products as often as possible.
- Develop a shared protocol for peer response to drafts.
- Use talk and drama as prewriting and during-writing support.

(continues)

FIGURE 1.1   Guidance document for academic-year professional development *(continued)*

Put conventions and test preparation in perspective
- Have explicit discussions about language diversity.
- Put more emphasis on inquiry-based language study rather than correction.
- Integrate test preparation with typical instruction.

Develop shared assessment tools/strategies for writing
- Adopt a school-wide prompt for on-demand writing that can be compared on various dimensions.
- Develop shared rubrics/expectations for portfolio pieces.
- Develop shared expectations for tracking individual progress.

Although some teachers reported integrating aspects from the PD into their practice, Robinson, like many urban schools, was pursuing multiple reform initiatives and program adoptions. Teachers struggled to address agendas that often felt unrelated. For this reason, the intensive, focused nature of the three-week institute was appealing to participants, as it would offer sustained time and support to experiment with and refine understandings of the high-utility approaches from the previous PD. It would also offer opportunities to construct new knowledge with colleagues, which many thought would be energizing.

Program Participants

The program included two different participant groups, the adults who were hired to staff it and the youth they taught.

Adult Staff

The Brown district used its standard processes for summer employment to advertise and fill staff positions in the institute. Each year the teams included four to eight teachers. The total varied with student enrollment and the availability of grant monies, but it was always an even number in anticipation of the paired co-teaching that was an essential element of the program. In Year 1 all six staff came from the Robinson English department. The Year 2 team included four English teachers from Robinson and two more who worked at a middle school feeder—a staffing move intended to spread principles and practices from the program further down the K–12 continuum. The hiring pool expanded even further in Years 3 and 4 to include Robinson teachers of social studies, English as a second language, and special education—again, in hopes of building capacity and common language for teaching writing across the disciplines. As indicated in table 1.1, more than half of the teachers participated in two or more iterations of the program. Staff cycled in and out based on personal commitments (e.g., getting married) and professional obligations (e.g., serving as the building administrator for summer school).

Teachers had between three and twenty years of experience, though most were in the first decade of their careers. Ten were female and two male. All, to my knowledge, were native English speakers, with eleven identifying as White and one as Native American. Such demographics were characteristic of the district, which struggled, as do many urban districts, to attract a teaching force matching the diversity of its student body.

In addition to these teachers and me, a number of other people contributed to the institute. The early college project hired Mary Taylor, a recently retired teacher leader from the Brown district, to serve as the liaison between the university and Robinson on several initiatives,

TABLE 1.1   Staff profiles

Pseudonym	Subjects Taught	Years Involved
Arlene	English	2
Crystal	Social Studies	3, 4
Cynthia	English	2
Jake	English	1, 2, 3, 4
Janice	English, Special Education	1, 2, 3, 4
Jimmy	English	2, 4
Joanna	Special Education	4
Kristina	English	2
Maddie	Social Studies, ESL	3, 4
Nicole	English	1
Rebecca	English	1, 4
Sue	English	1, 4

including but not limited to Years 1–3 of the institute. With assistance from graduate students Lauren Shallish, Carrie Rood, and Bridget Lawson, Mary dealt with logistical details such as arranging student transportation, reserving rooms, and communicating with families. When she had time, she also participated in planning, worked with students one-to-one, and occasionally co-taught during opening meetings. Bryan Crandall served as an unpaid assistant director in Year 1, helping me with the initial design, documenting meetings, and modeling practices such as conferring. In Year 3, when the Robinson team included just four teachers, I invited two master's students to pursue internships within the project as well: Paul Czuprynski, who was earning a certification in literacy education, and Lorraine Adu-Krow, who was pursuing certification in social studies education. Each was assigned to a teacher dyad, creating what we affectionately called the "triads" that year—Paul with Janice and Maddie, and Lorraine with Jake and Crystal.

Students

We initiated recruitment each year by sending an invitation to the permanent addresses of all students slated to attend Robinson as ninth graders in the fall. The letters were supplemented by presentations in eighth-grade classes at the three main feeder schools and home telephone calls by Mary Taylor and several graduate assistants. In Years 1 and 2 our target pool included just over three hundred students, which was then reduced to about one hundred in Year 3 when Robinson reorganized internally into three academies, each with some autonomy to develop programming with community partners. In Years 3 and 4 several staff members supplemented the roster of rising freshmen with targeted invitations to older students already enrolled at Robinson, mostly English learners, whom they thought might benefit. (Such an invitation is what brought us Ibrahim, whose personal narrative snippet at the beginning of the book recounts learning to read at age sixteen.)

As a result of these efforts, 62 students attended regularly in Year 1, 56 in Year 2, 27 in Year 3, and 45 in Year 4, for a total of 190. Their surveys and comments suggested they participated for varied reasons, some by choice and others under pressure to do so from teachers or family members. Some were avid writers seeking to develop their craft (one from Year 1 had already written a novel by the time he left middle school), others were fair-to-middling students who wanted to get off to a solid start in high school, and still others enrolled in hopes that the program might reduce their literacy struggles.

In terms of the demographics tracked by the state education department, institute participants were diverse on numerous fronts. The Year 1 cohort was 60 percent female and 40 percent male—a gender gap that improved to 53 percent and 47 percent, respectively, by Year 4. Each cohort included a mix of students from different race/ethnicity categories, with Black/African American girls typically representing the largest subgroup and White boys representing the smallest. The percentage of English language learners grew steadily, from about 15 percent in Year 1 to just under 50 percent in Year 4. This trend likely reflected two factors: (1) upticks in their representation in the overall school population from 13 percent in Year 1 to 22 percent by Year 4 and (2) targeted recruiting by Maddie and others mentioned earlier.

Even as I share these identity-related statistics, I am aware of the complications they represent. Such labels can be limiting and reductionist, particularly at a time when more and more people acknowledge categories such as race and gender as messy, shifting social constructions, not stable, agreed-upon realities. Yet the institute was designed around learner heterogeneity, and it yielded positive outcomes for students from groups that have not always been served well by school. My experience suggests that when many teachers encounter an example of strong student writing that is unmarked in terms of identity, they tend to assume dominant-group membership for the author. To interrupt this pattern, which renders students from predictable groups less visible than others, I typically include demographic information in my extended descriptions of students and their composing. I have also included a table in appendix A that summarizes what I knew about gender, race/ethnicity, language status, and the years of participation for all fifty-seven students that I feature by name in this book. Although these representational choices fail to capture Robinson youth's complexity, I hope they make learner variance discernible in positive ways, particularly when combined with the multiplicity and vitality of students' writing.

I did not include a column in the table to indicate students' disability status, because data in this category are not just complex to interpret but also incomplete. Because the institute was a voluntary summer enrichment program, not summer school, we had limited access to official school records. Neither the enrollment forms nor the first-day survey asked disability-related questions. It was not uncommon, however, for students or their family members to disclose such information to us informally by choice. In a few instances, institute staff members advocated for particular kinds of academic-year services to be made available for kids they knew in the summer who did not already have such designations. From these information sources, I can say that we worked with students whose disclosed disability labels included learning disabilities, autism, emotional disturbance, attention deficit disorder, and traumatic brain injury and that they represented about 15 percent of our student population each year. I mention individual participants' disability status, when known, in the chapters that follow for the same reasons that I discuss their gender, race/ethnicity, and language.

Program Overview

From the beginning the writing institute was framed with a dual set of related but not identical purposes. It was intended as enrichment, not remediation, for students and as professional development, not simply an employment opportunity, for adults.

For students it was designed to build academic writing skills and habits of mind that the early college team felt would serve as a strong foundation for entering students, including approaches to idea generation, organizational strategies, and a willingness to revise. A secondary, but still important, purpose was related to transitioning successfully to high school. Although Robinson's core constituency came from three schools located in the same geographic quadrant of the city as the high school, the freshman cohort in a given year always included students who attended eighth grade in numerous other schools in the district, as well as several private and parochial schools. Recruitment therefore emphasized the benefits of becoming oriented to the building layout and getting familiar with high school expectations. It also highlighted opportunities to build relationships with half a dozen teachers and make new friends before September classes.

For adults the program was meant to build capacity to teach writing to diverse populations that could be employed, at some point, in service of academic-year instruction. For this reason the program took place on the Robinson campus rather than on the university campus, and it drew on resources available to teachers such as no-frills free software that could be downloaded and used on Robinson's not-so-new computers. And, finally, it drew its primary teaching staff from Brown personnel.

May and June Preparation

Once Robinson administrators made decisions about which staff applicants would be hired, I assigned co-teaching dyads based on what I knew about each person. To provide more opportunities for professional growth to the adults and more diversity of approaches for the students, I sought to create teams that would allow individuals to complement and not duplicate each other's strengths. In Years 2 through 4, I paired returning staff as much as possible with newcomers in order to support the latter in becoming familiar with the program's goals and structures. A mix of new and veteran staff was ideal, balancing institutional memory with fresh perspectives on how to approach persistent instructional problems.

The terms for staff participation called for ten hours of planning and professional development in May and June, prior to the program's start with youth in July. In Year 1 these ten hours of work yielded the basic architecture of the program, including the two essential questions, the daily schedule, and the selection of personal narratives and digital stories as the two focal genres students would produce. We also agreed that both students and teachers would use writer's notebooks regularly. Most discussions took place as a full team, but time was also allotted for co-teaching dyads to establish working relationships.

During subsequent iterations, we retained the pre-program planning and team-building activities, although in several years we reduced the number of sessions from five to four to accommodate difficulties in identifying slots when everyone could be available during hectic end-of-year schedules. From Year 2 on, we also devoted more time during May and June to constructing our own digital stories for use as models with students and to identifying community guests to make presentations about writing in their personal and professional lives (more on this in chapter 5).

Daily Schedule of Activities

The program took place over three weeks each July, Monday through Friday. Teachers reported each day by 8:30 a.m. so that they could use the thirty-minute period prior to students' arrival at 9:00 a.m. for setup, announcements, and check-ins with co-teachers. Instruction with youth took place from 9 a.m. to noon. From noon to 2:30 p.m., after students' departure, staff members convened to debrief on the day's activities, review student work, and plan subsequent lessons. (I discuss these afternoon sessions and their relationship to our May and June planning more thoroughly in chapter 2.)

Each instructional period began with a thirty-to-forty-minute opening meeting in the LGIR, the same space where the end-of-program celebration took place. Pairs of teachers facilitated the meeting each day, sometimes in their assigned co-teaching dyads and sometimes with other colleagues. Instruction at this time typically involved a warm-up prompt for the writer's notebook followed by a lesson introducing or reinforcing skills that students would apply to their personal narratives or digital stories during dyad-supervised composing time later in the day. Every few days the opening meeting was extended to an hour to accommodate an invited presentation by a guest writer from the community and a question-and-answer period with the audience. Staff members who were not assigned to facilitate opening meeting spread out across the LGIR, observing and taking notes, providing support to students as needed, and participating in the tasks themselves.

For the next sixty to one hundred minutes of each day, students moved into smaller groups, each led by a co-teaching dyad. We constructed these groups on the Tuesday afternoon of our first week together, after we had two days to interact with students, and we took care to balance them along variables such as sending school, gender, race/ethnicity, first language, perceived gregariousness, and writing skill as revealed by our first several tasks. Dyad groups met either in a classroom or in a designated computer lab, depending on the activity and the availability of the latter. (We sometimes had to share Robinson's three labs with other programs running concurrently, including summer school.) Co-teachers implemented collective plans devised by the full staff during afternoon planning sessions. Typical activities included discussion of exemplar texts in the focal genres, topic brainstorming, internet research related to digital story topics, drafting, peer feedback, and teacher conferences.

The dyad portion of the day also included snack and "15-15," a term we coined for our expectation that students in the program would complete fifteen consecutive days of at least fifteen minutes of independent reading in a book that many selected from Robinson's summer reading lists. Kids typically sipped water and noshed on chips or granola bars while reading. Beginning in Year 2, students logged their daily progress in a chart taped to the inside cover of their writer's notebook. Across all four years, staff members invited students to make connections between the aspects of writer's craft they observed in their 15-15 books and the writing they were simultaneously pursuing, particularly their personal narratives. Sometimes they shared these connections orally with the group; on other occasions, they noted their impressions on sticky notes and posted these in the classrooms.

The last twenty minutes of each day were spent back in the LGIR for a whole-program closing meeting, during which we previewed upcoming events, including our guest visits, and shared samples of strong student work in progress. Closing meetings on Fridays typically involved guided reflection activities, including page counts of writer's notebook production, and the distribution of Popsicles before students scattered to walk home or catch a public bus, with fares paid by the district. On the last day of each year's program, we shortened each instructional component to allow for a ninety-minute public celebration as described in the introduction.

How Did We Know It Worked?

Over four years my collaborators and I gathered a wide range of data to assess the institute's effectiveness, make adjustments, and inform our research recommendations. These data included the following:

- agendas, handouts, and meeting notes from planning sessions in May and June
- plans, materials, and observational notes for fifteen days of instruction in July
- plans and meeting notes from fifteen afternoon planning sessions in July
- copies of students' writer's notebooks
- copies of draft materials and final versions of personal narratives and digital stories
- photographs of classroom space and resources and of teachers and students interacting with each other
- daily reflective journal entries I made as institute director and primary research investigator
- forty-to-sixty-minute individual interviews I conducted with staff members several months after each iteration concluded

The comprehensiveness of this data set allowed my collaborators and me to make inferences that the program worked well, for both students and adults, in light of our related but distinct pedagogical goals for both groups. As I address particular components of the program in subsequent chapters, I will share many examples of these data to support and illustrate my assertions. In this introductory chapter, however, let me share some broad indicators of success to demonstrate why it's worth reading on to learn more.

Several important indicators of student satisfaction with the program, particularly given its voluntary nature, had to do with attendance and involvement. Despite the competing attractions of attending athletic camps, hanging out at the local pool, playing video games, and sleeping in, the majority of our kids showed up, day after day, ready to engage (including some whose school-year profile was decidedly different, according to staff members who knew them already). The strong turnout of friends and family members at each end-of-program celebration was another data point we used as a proxy for impact. As Arlene explained following Year 2, "You can see that they were invested in . . . and proud of their work" based on how many of them "got their adults to come." On a couple of occasions, students even finagled extra bus passes from the program to fund the presence of older siblings when parents could not be available, suggesting how important it was for someone close to them to view their work. Over time some faces at the celebration became familiar, as at least nine families sent multiple children to participate in successive iterations. (One family, the Mukendis, sent three children—two girls and a boy—in different years, all of whom chose to write personal narratives about the family's migration from Congo with interesting variations in their perspectives that were likely associated with gender and age.) That kids elected to attend the program consistently, with support from home, was an important indicator of the program's value to the Robinson community.

Another indicator that the program was meeting its pedagogical goals for students was the quality of the products they created, particularly in the two focal genres. Although we did not see it as appropriate to score or grade students' final versions of their narratives or their digital stories within the context of a voluntary enrichment program, we did review those work samples as a team each year to note strengths and weaknesses and to identify potential teaching points for subsequent iterations. Several patterns struck us during these reviews over time, including better development with details for the personal narratives and greater coherence related to the essential questions for the digital stories. The increases in quality from year to year were modest, but they coincided with overall reductions in initial skill and experience levels in our student population, suggesting improvements in our ability to design instruction to address varied student learning needs.

Exit surveys represented additional information about the program's impact on students. (See figure 1.2 for a completed example from Ayaan, a Somali-born girl who spoke three languages.) The surveys revealed numerous patterns, some about writing outcomes and some about our transition goals for ninth grade. During Year 4, for instance, students' average rating for their level of agreement with the statement "I am confident in my ability to write a complete essay" jumped nearly a full point on a 5-point scale, from 4.08 on Day 1 to 4.94 on Day 15. The increases associated with "I am confident in using technology to tell a story" and "I can use other people's good writing as a model to improve my own" were nearly as large (.69 and .77, respectively). At the end of the program, 88 percent of students reported making a personal connection to at least one teacher, with 92 percent reporting they had made either "a lot" or "a couple" of new friends. And every single respondent assigned the highest possible rating of agreement to the final item: "I expect to be successful academically during my 9th grade year." Although the small sample size suggests a need for caution in making claims from these data, the patterns are clearly promising, especially when combined with other information.

The teacher indicators were similarly positive. Like students, adults voted with their feet: the staff for each iteration arrived early, stayed late, and, in many cases, returned for additional years of service. In Years 3 and 4, when changes in Robinson's academy structure reduced the pool of rising ninth graders we could serve, staff members sought and received permission to recruit selected upper-class students from their academic-year classes in order to make an experience they valued available to more students. In their interviews, they spoke clearly about the value of their participation, using superlatives like the following:

- It was probably my best teaching experience in this district, ever. (Cynthia)
- That will be the ideal if we could somehow have our school year look like our summer. Imagine the amount of work that would get done. (Janice)

FIGURE 1.2 Ayaan's completed exit survey

Name _____

Exit Survey: 2013 Summer Writing Institute

1. What are the three most important things you learned during the summer institute? Explain.

a. It very important to write because writing can take you anywhere and it represents you.

b. I learned to ~~meet~~ meet new people because when I first came to the writing institute I didn't know most of the people here so I meet alot of peop

c. I learned that you are going to have to write through out your life so it would be better to get use to it now better then later

2. What were your favorite parts of the summer institute? Tell us what you liked about them.

My favorite parts of the summer institute was when we went in the computer lab and wrote a persona Narrative and when we got into grou and made our digital stories. ~~What I like~~ What I like about them was because we got to write about ~~ourse~~ ourself an people get to read them.

3. As a result of participating in the summer institute, my writing has (circle one):

(improved a lot)   improved a little   stayed the same

4. I enjoyed working on my (circle all that apply):

(writer's notebook)   (personal narrative   digital story)

FIGURE 1.2   Ayaan's completed exit survey *(continued)*

Please rate the following statements using the five-point scale:

1 = Strongly Disagree   2 = Disagree   3 = Neutral   4 = Agree   5 = Strongly Agree

Please circle your choice.

Statement	Rating
1. I am confident in my ability to write every day.	1 2 3 4 (5)
2. I am confident in my ability to write a complete essay.	1 2 3 4 (5)
3. I am confident in writing about myself.	1 2 3 4 (5)
4. I am confident in using technology to tell a story.	1 2 3 4 (5)
5. I am confident in my ability to include a variety of interesting details in my writing and text.	1 2 3 4 (5)
6. I can use other people's good writing as a model to improve my own.	1 2 3 4 (5)
7. I am comfortable sharing my writing with other people.	1 2 3 4 (5)
8. I can give good feedback to other people on their writing.	1 2 3 4 (5)
9. My writing has good overall organization.	1 2 3 4 (5)
10. I am good at focusing my writing on a main idea.	1 2 3 4 (5)
11. I can clearly express the purpose of my written text.	1 2 3 4 (5)
12. I expect to do well in English 9 next year.	1 2 3 4 (5)
13. I expect to be able to write well for all of my classes in high school.	1 2 3 4 (5)
14. I expect to be successful academically during my 9th grade year.	1 2 3 4 (5)

5. Circle the response for each of the following items that best reflects your thinking:

   a. I made some new friends during the summer institute.

   (A lot of them)   A couple   None

   b. I enjoyed having time to read a book of my choosing.

   (Yes)   Somewhat   Not at all

   c. I made a personal connection to teachers during the institute.

   (Yes, to several)   Yes, to one   Not at all

- My favorite experience yet. . . . The team planning, the orchestration of it—the way you had everybody sitting there and throwing ideas out, writing it down, putting it back. . . . If teachers could be pushed to do that, or given time to do that, on a regular basis, what a beautiful job teaching would be. (Kristina)

Although our research design was admittedly focused on understanding and improving the program over time rather than gauging its impact on academic-year instruction, we collected data each year that suggested that participation made a difference to teachers. Nearly every teacher recounted productive post-institute interactions with youth who participated, ranging from daily check-in visits from students not on their rosters (Janice, Jake, Arlene) to one student's volunteering to share his digital story from the summer with his classmates to help model the genre in class (Sue). In addition, every teacher reported importing specific instructional tools or routines from the summer into their regular practice. Cynthia, for example, recommitted to regular use of writer's notebooks with students, even though she moved to another school in the year following her participation on staff. Jake admitted, with pride and a little sheepishness, that he had "become really big on modeling" writing processes, after two years of arguing that such a practice would lead to his students simply replicating his text. Crystal shared that her post-institute social studies classes focused "a lot more on process, breaking things down step by step," and that she had not only created new demonstration lessons and assignment checklists but also hosted after-school writing workshops to confer with students seeking additional assistance. Of course I recognize the limitations of such self-reported data, and nearly all teachers acknowledged, on their own, that their ability to enact institute principles and practices during the school year was blunted by such factors as isolation, competing reform initiatives, and time constraints. Still, the convergence in how a diverse group of professionals talked about their common experience, both how they experienced it and how they applied their learning later, suggests a high degree of impact and meaning for them derived from a model worth interrogating.

CHAPTER 2

Collaborative Planning for Writing Instruction

It's Friday, Day 5 of Year 1, and the kids are gone. In the back of the LGIR, two tables are pushed together to form a square. Everyone on staff but me is seated around it, lunch containers pushed to the side. I am standing at the whiteboard, recording everyone's contributions. The board is divided into two halves, one with an emerging plan for Monday and the other for longer-term plans. Both halves are littered with cross-outs, arrows to indicate new sequencing, and carets for last-minute additions. Assistant director Bryan Crandall is doing his best to transfer the notes into a lesson plan template on his laptop.

As the whiteboard gets messier, Janice comments that it resembles the chalkboard that Russell Crowe's character uses in the film *A Beautiful Mind* to tackle complex math problems while managing his mental health. The group finds this connection apt, particularly when someone points out that Bryan, who is usually tolerant of messiness and ambiguity, is struggling to keep up with my scrawl, while I, usually neat and organized in my note taking, revel in the disorder. We joke that we are all adopting one another's characteristics from working so closely together. Later I will edit Bryan's document for clarity and then email it to the staff for review. On Monday morning individuals will annotate hard copies during check-ins with their teaching partners just before students arrive.

Over the next three years, the exchange about the Crowe film will become part of the program's lexicon, shorthand for describing our collaborative planning process. Teachers not on the inaugural staff will still reference that moment, describing pending instructional decisions to others with comments like this: "Yeah, we need to figure that out. Don't worry—we'll 'beautiful-mind' it this afternoon." In a reflective interview, Billy remembered:

> That is the first thing I picture: you up at the whiteboard . . . somebody saying something and then somebody else using that and everybody spit-balling ideas off of each other. Tremendous amounts of dialogue, total immersion from everybody in an idea, and respect for each other. . . . Everybody had equal say, everybody contributed as far as planning the direction of the lessons. And then in terms of the instruction, you know, I think it showed because everybody knew where we were going.

I begin my discussion of teachers' collaborative planning with this scene and Billy's comments because they suggest fundamental ideas about the institute, including our development of routines and tools for working together, the esprit de corps engendered by that work, and the instructional quality such coherence yielded. In the first section I describe what I call "big-picture planning," the tools and processes staff used to select focal genres, set learning objectives, and sequence the curriculum. This work was primarily done during after-school sessions in May and June, once the staff for a given year had been hired but before implementation with a new student cohort. In the second section I describe the tools and processes we used to translate big-picture plans into daily instruction during afternoon sessions while the program ran in July. I argue across the chapter that the interplay between big-picture and daily planning, as well as a process that drew on everyone's insights while burdening no one, supported staff in productively addressing learner differences.

Why We Embraced Teacher Collaboration

That Robinson teachers would embrace collaboration on writing instruction was not a foregone conclusion when leaders in the early college partnership and I began planning the institute's first iteration. In the backdrop for our work was the fact that several generations of American teachers, particularly those working in under-resourced schools, had been subjected to scripted curriculum as a control mechanism during politically motivated pendulum swings toward accountability.[1] Such mandates eroded teacher autonomy and morale while yielding limited literacy gains for students. Robinson teachers were thus understandably skeptical about new reform initiatives that might curtail their decision-making and perhaps fade away before full implementation anyway, as often happens with school change in urban contexts.[2]

The professional freedom that Robinson teachers craved came at some cost, however, even when they could achieve it. Inconsistent access to high-quality curriculum from the district left many working overtime to create their own materials while juggling the demands of managing classrooms, interacting with youth and their families, and responding to student work. Robinson had at least six levels of English for ninth graders, including one designated as pre–advanced placement, a computer-aided remediation class, and self-contained sections for students labeled with certain disabilities or as new English learners. This elaborate tracking system required preparation time to create separate plans for each level, impeded teachers' ability to share effective approaches and assignments with one another, and diverted time and energy to assigning (and reassigning) students to the "right" level rather than addressing other factors that might support greater success. Many teachers had personal experience with subject-area or interdisciplinary team meetings that led to time-consuming project planning at best and devolved into gossip sessions about individual kids at worst. Navigating these complexities created fatigue and frustration.

The professional literature on teaching writing did not offer much additional insight about leveraging collaboration to address inequitable outcomes for learners. Some of the best-known authors taught populations that were quite culturally and linguistically homogeneous, making their recommendations less credible and compelling to Robinson teachers.[3] Other authors had more diverse student rosters, but their descriptions of classroom practice offered little insight about working with the push-in teaching partners in special education and English as a new language (ENL), who were increasingly present in inclusive classes.[4] Teaching writing was often presented as a solo endeavor in the most popular practitioner resources.

Yet a growing body of literature on successful school reform in urban contexts suggested that teacher collaboration could lever change, benefiting student engagement and achievement when sustained over time and focused on instruction. In a groundbreaking study across four states, Judith Langer documented the characteristics of middle and high schools that were "beating the odds," supporting English achievement for their students at higher rates than demographically similar populations.[5] Teachers in higher-performing schools collaborated with one another and with school leaders to analyze the tests to which they were accountable and then design lessons that integrated those skills into existing curriculum rather than treating test preparation as an add-on. Profiles of districts that reduced achievement gaps for low-income and minority students also revealed the importance of teachers' collective work in developing coherent curricula and consensus based on high expectations.[6] And when Marc Tucker and his colleagues at the National Center on Education and the Economy profiled five educational systems outperforming the United States on international assessments and equity measures, nearly all of those systems featured systematic supports for teachers to work together on designing curriculum, instruction, and assessment.[7] Although writing rarely received as much attention in these reports as reading or literacy defined broadly, it seemed reasonable to conjecture that high-quality, well-theorized teacher collaboration might enhance writing instruction for diverse student populations.

The convergence of these emerging findings and Robinson staff's desire to interrupt the status quo for themselves and their students created opportunity to explore different ways of working together. The summer writing institute became a space where we could experiment with different instructional conditions and assumptions but with the same students we were all committed to serving better. This work involved the use of both "big-picture" tools and processes as well as daily ones.

Big-Picture Tools for Teacher Collaboration

Although Billy's reminiscence focused on afternoon planning in July, program-related collaboration began earlier than that. Prior to Year 1, Robinson administrators agreed to pay the teachers who staffed the institute for up to ten hours of pre-program planning. This work was seen by all of us as necessary for co-constructing a program that would address our goals for both adolescent and adult learners. Everyone was clear that the institute's architecture needed to draw on research as well as Robinson teachers' knowledge of students and the local context—a hybrid design that could only be created through sustained collaboration.

To this end we scheduled five planning sessions in May and June before the launch of the Year 1 program with students. The two-hour sessions took place after school about once a week. As facilitator, I devised a plan for each meeting, with proposed activities and time frames. Over time, as the group grew more comfortable with co-designing what staff member Rebecca called "a new learning opportunity and a place for collaboration," my plans became more provisional, with some items abandoned and others—such as the 15-15 component linking the institute to Robinson's summer reading requirements—expanded because of teacher interest.

During Year 1 we made some decisions retained across four iterations, including division of the daily three-hour instructional period into the predictable chunks described in chapter 1 and selection of the program-wide essential questions discussed in chapter 3. We also established some habits for documenting our thinking, such as brainstorming ideas on chart paper that we saved and displayed each time we met. This practice validated contributions from multiple team members and helped the sessions build coherently. On occasion, the ability to revisit an idea from an earlier conversation helped us to move past a planning logjam.

Two other important tasks were the selection of focal genres, with an accompanying set of learning objectives, and the development of fifteen-day graphic organizers to help us sequence and organize instruction with those objectives in mind. Each is discussed next.

Selection of Focal Genres

To present writing as a powerful tool with varied purposes, we decided that students would produce two texts representing different aspects of contemporary composing. One text was a 500-to-750-word personal narrative that students would polish via multiple revisions. We felt that this product would help us get to know students personally, which would improve our ability to coach and support them, and that focusing on persistence and revision would extend but not duplicate student experiences from middle school. The second text, a digital story of two to four minutes on a topic of interest related to the essential questions, would be authored in groups of two or three, allowing students to compose with multimedia and practice collaborative authorship. We thought that using technology would be appealing to many students and help identify the institute with enrichment rather than remediation discourses. Our choice of these products also allowed us to attend to two of the three text types and forms featured in the Common Core Standards, which were receiving considerable attention in district- and regional-level PD at the time.

With our genre choices settled, we needed to narrow the instructional focus further. Each product offered adolescent writers too many learning opportunities to address thoroughly in a fifteen-day program. To make such decisions, we combined brainstorming and discussion at the assigned team level with debriefing and decision-making as a full staff, as demonstrated by this excerpt from a May session plan:

- Pose this question: *If we're asking students to create digital stories that will require inquiry and research, what skills and strategies will we need to teach over the three weeks so that kids can do these things at a high level?*
- Brainstorm initial lists in dyads and then make group list together.
- Emphasize at the end of that list-making that some kids will have some of these skills already, so we need to have a differentiated plan for supporting them, and that having a multi-teacher team will help in this regard.

In subsequent meetings we repeated this process for personal narratives and for writer's notebooks, which students would use to support construction of both focal genres. Between sessions I typed and made copies of the group notes for subsequent review and editing. Eventually we achieved consensus on the learning objectives shown in figure 2.1.

Although both the focal genres and the objectives remained consistent across four iterations, we did make some adjustments in how we prepared to address them with students. The most significant adjustment related to digital stories. In Year 1 our big-picture planning sessions included discussion of our digital story expectations, including that staff members would create examples of their own to share with students. But we did not devote any time during May or June to our own composing, leaving individuals to construct exemplars on their own time or during moments stolen from already jam-packed planning in July. This meant that only some staff members had digital stories they could draw on instructionally. This snag was raised during our final Year 1 debriefing,

FIGURE 2.1   Learning objectives

Product	Objective
Writer's Notebook	• Developing fluency • Generating ideas • Using short bursts of writing to develop more sustained pieces • Taking notes
Personal Narrative	• Finding a satisfying topic • Writing powerful leads • Adding sensory details (but not too many) • Addressing the "So what?" question
Digital Stories	• Using a planning tool integrating attention to narrated text, images, and audio • Connecting personal interests to common essential questions • Rehearsing narration for fluent delivery • Writing credits of various kinds
Overall	• Developing a positive disposition toward revision • Learning to provide and use specific feedback

when Sue suggested that we "consult with the librarian next time about our technology" and Janice proposed that "teacher teams should have completed projects before they set out to teach digital story telling."

In Year 2 we reserved a computer lab for two of our big-picture planning sessions. Our agendas included time for staff to construct their own digital stories using a free tool, Photo Story 3, that Gretchen, the Robinson librarian, recommended to us as friendlier than the tool we used initially (Microsoft PowerPoint). At the end of each work period, we reflected on our progress and then debriefed as a team. We used this sequence—compose, reflect, debrief—consistently from then on to support staff creation of digital stories. We also invited Gretchen to help troubleshoot problems with saving to teachers' school computer hard drives, using the microphones to audiotape narration, and importing music files for the stories' soundtracks. These adjustments ensured that both focal genres, not just the narratives, were addressed rigorously in our planning and, eventually, in our modeling. (See chapter 5 for more on this.)

Fifteen-Day Organizers

We knew that it was ambitious to expect everyone in a heterogeneous group of rising ninth graders to construct both focal genres in a fifteen-day program. Unlike academic-year units, where teachers can often adjust a due date if needed, the institute had a hard stop: on the third Friday, students would walk out the door. To achieve closure and launch students at Robinson with confidence, it was important that each student complete both products satisfactorily. This was especially true for students with disabilities and English language learners (ELLs) in order to avoid reinforcing deficit-oriented stereotypes about their capabilities. Concerns about supporting all students adequately within a compressed format led us to develop what became a central tool of the program—the fifteen-day organizer.

To build the organizer, I created a one-page handout with the days of the week across the top and Weeks 1, 2, and 3 down the side. During a big-picture planning session, individual staff members recorded ideas about what lessons needed to be taught and when, given our learning objectives for digital stories. They met with their assigned teaching partners to combine and refine their suggestions (see figure 2.2 for a sample from Jake and Janice) and then repeated the procedure for personal narratives.

At session's end I collected the set of documents to create a master organizer reflecting contributions from all three dyads. To keep track of which proposed lessons applied to which genre, I color coded references to each, using red font for personal narratives and green for digital stories. I brought copies of the new organizer for staff review at our next planning meeting. After some light edits, mostly focused on aligning work in the writer's notebooks with the two focal genres, we began using the organizer to guide more detailed daily planning.

This first version of the fifteen-day organizer turned out to be remarkably stable. We reviewed it during big-picture planning over the next three years, making enough changes to call it a living document but not so many that they threatened the Year 1 team's vision. The most significant change was between Year 1 and Year 2, when we adjusted time allocations for the focal genres. We originally envisioned that each day would have a roughly equivalent chunk of time devoted to each genre. As we translated the organizer into daily practice, however, the transitions from one product to another often felt awkward. We settled

FIGURE 2.2 Completed brainstorming template

Overview of Digital Storytelling Group Projects: What Needs to Happen When?

	Monday	Tuesday	Wednesday	Thursday	Friday
W E E K 1	survey	letter	student sample __ Intro D.S. project	"getting started" skills: 1) pick an inquiry 2) listing sources of info.	cooperative learning: assign responsibility MODEL
		← E.Q.'s discussion →		↕	
W E E K 2	(INFO GATHERING) ----> ORGANIZE thoughts/content ★ trusted sources ★ note taking / outlining (interview skills for those who need it)		critique feedback ⟩ how to...	Narrative Voice-Over Instruction	Story boarding
W E E K 3	(Production Begins) → tech: import graphics program ----> ★ vocal performance -critique		FINAL EDIT + test run (peer feedback) ↗ Save to Drive or disk		← Presentation of D.S.

into attending more thoroughly to the personal narrative during the first week and to the digital story in the third week, with the second week serving as a transition between them. This distribution of emphasis worked well, so we retained it going forward. (See appendix B for the Year 4 organizer.)

Once the organizer was developed, we used it to build capacity for collaborative teaching. Most staff in Year 1 and beyond reported at least a little co-teaching experience, but it was variable in organization and quality. Some had worked with partners who interacted solely with students identified with disabilities, support that sometimes isolated those students from their peers. Some had co-teachers but little or no planning time, which often relegated the push-in professional to an assistant who repeated directions and managed behavior. One or two of them had worked in contexts where both partners planned and implemented instruction for shared students, but such scenarios were rare and vulnerable to scheduling vagaries. To address this variability and offer more robust co-teaching possibilities within the institute, I sought assistance in Year 1 from Janice, who was dually certified in English and special education and had extensive experience working with other professionals. She developed and led an interactive workshop during a planning session that presented the benefits of co-teaching, described six common configurations,[8] and proposed discussion prompts to help teams negotiate a mutually comfortable approach.

After Janice's overview, I asked each dyad to sit together to make notes about where they could envision employing the co-teaching configurations across the fifteen-day organizer. These conversations served several important purposes. First, they gave the staff a chance to explore and apply the co-teaching configurations Janice presented, particularly those such as station teaching that were less commonly used at Robinson. The direction to consider at least three different configurations reinforced the idea that co-teaching in the institute would be varied. Second, the conversations about the organizer strengthened the dyads as individuals shared their previous experiences with teaching partners and emerging understandings of how we would all work together. Such an information exchange was crucial to establishing the relationships on which successful co-teaching depends.

Post-program interviews revealed that staff clearly valued the opportunity to build rapport and consensus with new teaching partners that would allow them to work together with what Jake described as "seamlessness." Janice's co-teaching workshop became a fixture in our big-picture planning, repeated during the next three iterations, each of which saw returning staff members but never the same combinations for co-teaching dyads. That session positioned us well for the intensive work of designing and refining daily plans to bring the fifteen-day organizer to life with students.

Daily Tools for Teacher Collaboration

The most intensive teacher collaboration in the institute took place after students left class each day and the staff commenced afternoon planning. During this time, we used three tools routinely: (1) professional writing prompts, (2) common plans, and (3) review of student work. Figure 2.3 overviews one session to demonstrate how these tools were typically sequenced.

Before I discuss each daily tool, let me note the relationship between them and big-picture planning. Construction of a single plan was always informed by the fifteen-day organizer. Review of student work was always informed by the learning objectives pasted at the bottom of the fifteen-day organizer and by understandings of the focal genres constructed during May and June. Key to the institute's success was this shared sense of purpose—described previously by Billy as everybody

FIGURE 2.3   Sample plan for afternoon collaborative session

Afternoon Plan: Day 7

12:15–12:40	Time for writer's notebooks with this prompt: "Write about something that made you think today, as a teacher of writing, and why." Share out across the group; everyone contributes
12:40–1:00	Debriefing about opening/closing meeting: • What's working? • What needs tweaking?
1:00–1:45	Each dyad reads notebooks and narrative drafts for their students • Make notes on sticky notes about next steps for each kid
1:45–2:30	Construct Day 8 plan together on whiteboard

knowing "where we were going"—combined with ongoing dialogue structured by the daily tools.

Professional Writing Prompts

Nearly every afternoon session over four years began with five to ten minutes of silent writing by all staff, including me. This writing was guided by an open-ended prompt, followed by an invitation for individuals to share ideas from that writing in a discussion lasting another ten to twenty minutes, depending on the topic and other agenda items. Prompts reflected different purposes, including (1) to promote reflection by individual teachers about their practice, (2) to generate ideas to inform future planning, (3) to capture informal assessment data, and (4) to focus attention on a student or students. Some prompts were designed to spotlight what kids had learned with reference to the objectives as opposed to whether they had participated or engaged. Others were intended to surface discussion about which youth were most on teachers' radar screens, for what reasons, and in some cases, to interrupt those patterns. Figure 2.4 includes a sampling of prompts from Year 4 to illustrate the range.

Sharing sparked by the writing was also varied. On some days staff summarized main ideas from their entries orally; on other days they identified and read a single sentence to spark further discussion. Only rarely did anyone read an entire entry, which seemed too time-consuming for the planning traction it might produce. We framed reflective writing as a rehearsal tool for collaborative planning and decision-making, not an end in itself.

The combination of writing and debriefing raised important ideas for group consideration. For example, when several adults wrote about the same student, Kiara, but reported varying degrees of success in supporting her sustained generation of text, we could analyze the costs and benefits of different approaches for supporting student independence. When girls were disproportionately represented in the list of students with whom staff reported meaningful interactions on a given day, we could examine how to adjust our lenses to ensure more gender equity. And when a positive trend was raised by more than one staff member—for instance, students' increased ability to write inviting openings—it nudged us to make explicit and reflect on the instruction supporting that outcome. Such discussion emphasized teacher agency and careful

FIGURE 2.4   Sample writing prompts

Day	Prompt
1	Write about your first day impressions.
3	Write about: • the best aspect of co-teaching with your dyad partner today, and why • an adjustment you will make related to your co-teaching today, and why
6	Write about a conference you had today that moved a kid forward. Why was it helpful?
8	Today felt messier than usual—let's write about that. What didn't work so well? Let's "speak our bitterness" and move on.
9	Write about something you noticed today about a particular kid's learning or engagement. What was important about it? Choose a kid about whom you haven't thought or written as much so far.
10	Write about a digital story group that interested you today for some reason. Get down as much as you can about that group in 5 minutes.
13	Write about a moment today with a kid that pleasantly surprised you, and why.
15	Make two lists: • best aspects of the three weeks for you • things you can transfer to your work in the fall

planning rather than locating a trend in students' ability, effort, or personality. Writing-fueled talk thus promoted collective accountability for adults for the quality of student learning without targeting any one teacher.

Writing to spark discussion had other benefits related to equity within our own team. It increased the chances of all staff members contributing rather than privileging the voices of just a few. By Year 4 the potential for such privileging was evident. For instance, as the only four-year staff members, Jake and Janice had deeper reservoirs of memory and tradition on which to draw than those participating for the first time. It was tempting for others to defer to them and to me when we made "This is how we did it before" suggestions, even if those suggestions had not yet been tweaked to address current students' needs. In addition, English-certified staff members tended to be positioned differently than those with social studies or ENL backgrounds because of assumptions, especially early in each iteration, that English teaching required more expertise with writing instruction than other areas. Yet everyone around the table tended to be willing to share ideas in response to a prompt, even if they were otherwise reticent to speak up. (This was true even of Sue, a staff member in Years 1 and 4 who expressed her discomfort with group planning so bluntly that it launched a running joke among us.) Writing to plan also discouraged premature resolution of instructional challenges, particularly when I was deliberate in my role as facilitator about asking everyone to reread their entries for ideas not yet inserted into the conversation before moving on. Writing helped ensure that our planning drew equitably on insights across the group.

In addition to writing intended to benefit students, we also used notebook prompts to promote adult learning. Each staff member set a professional goal for institute participation. The goals varied, as this sampling reveals:

- Provide daily, diverse, and in-depth feedback to students (Billy)
- Support ELL students in acquiring new vocabulary and strategies (Joanna)
- Learn professional vocabulary around writing instruction from collaborators and use it consistently with students (Crystal)
- Support other colleagues' co-teaching, especially with kids who are struggling (Janice)

Goals were shared publicly so that the group could brainstorm possible support mechanisms to help each member achieve them. This process often linked one iteration to another because of the presence of returning staff. For example, Maddie related that her Year 4 goal about guiding but not dominating students' revision was inspired by Janice's similar goal the year before. Janice reminded Maddie that resolving not to accept "I don't know" from students in Year 3 had slowed down her writing conferences, reducing her tendency to solve students' problems for them herself, and she suggested that Maddie do the same. Other items in Maddie's support plan included her own proposal to ask five questions for each statement she made and Crystal's idea to offer exemplar texts as models rather than suggesting particular revisions.

Once such plans were in place, we typically devoted part of our Friday afternoon sessions to goal-related reflective writing. On some occasions this writing launched extensive group discussion; on other days the entries served as personal check-ins before we planned for the following week. Either way, the writing helped to periodically reset staff attention on their goals so that they did not get lost as the program's end neared and pressure to help students complete products intensified.

Common Plans

Another essential element of the institute was the use of common plans. I conjectured that the benefits associated with enacting one plan representing the best of everyone's thinking would be worth the corresponding constraint on creativity and autonomy for individual teachers. Focal genres and the fifteen-day organizer were important, but we still needed detailed daily plans for implementation by up to eight people working collaboratively. Unfortunately, none of us had a template before Year 1 that was up to the task.

The biggest limitation of the existing templates was their failure to account for the presence of multiple adults. Because we intended to enact several kinds of co-teaching across multiple instructional spaces, we needed a template that would communicate a good deal of information with efficiency. The balance was delicate: too much detail, and the plan would be unwieldy; too little, and staff members would be left to improvise on their own in ways that might threaten our collective vision.

To this end we developed a five-column format for the main section of the daily plan that addressed time, activities, location, personnel, and materials, as shown in the example in figure 2.5. Alignment across the columns increased the chances that designated teachers would be clear about their roles, that they would have the materials they needed, and that we would stay at least roughly on schedule.

A few days into Year 1, we added another feature to the template: a to-do list at the beginning. Typical tasks included materials creation, setup, and technological troubleshooting, as this example demonstrates:

- Distribute writer's notebooks to students' chairs in the LGIR. (all 3 teaching teams)
- Enlist kids to work on thank-you notes for guests. (Kelly)
- Get technology setup running by 8:40 at latest. (Cynthia)
- Get music playing for entrance. (Jake)
- Make copies of checklist for personal narratives. (Mary)

Dividing these tasks became part of afternoon planning, with individuals or dyads volunteering based on availability or skills. Collective guilt

FIGURE 2.5 Sample section of daily plan

Time	Activity	Location	Personnel	Materials
11:40–12:00	Closing Meeting: Show Billy's digital story and have them record noticings in notebooks Give them his script to review and ask them to add more items to the noticings, based on the script Show digital story about spoken-word poetry and lead students in completing two-column chart together: *What strengths do you notice? What suggestions for improvement would you make?* Complete 2 more lines, one for each digital story, in their EQ chart	LGIR	Mary facilitating & Kelly recording student ideas	YouTube video cued Script copies Jump drive with Year 1 digital stories on it Copy of EQ chart for document camera

also played a role in this process, as staff members sometimes took on less desirable assignments with a sigh and a comment such as "I'll do it—I haven't had a job in a couple of days."

Having a common daily template enhanced our ability to work together. The plans offered group-developed guidance for instruction to be carried out in real time, such as this note from the dyad portion of a Year 1, Day 8 plan:

Midway through [the work period], do a quick mini-lesson (<10 minutes) focusing kids on something that will improve their personal narratives OTHER THAN LEADS, which we'll deal with early next week, and then have them return to their drafts to try out what we've modeled and continue with their writing from there.

Possible areas of focus could include:

- dialogue
- making sure the piece has a point, answering the "So what?" question
- paragraphing
- providing concrete, specific, vivid details

The bulleted options reflected the group's best predictions about what would be beneficial to students given the learning objectives and priorities communicated in the fifteen-day organizer, as well as our review of student work from previous days. But the ultimate choice of what to highlight in the mini-lesson would be made by each teacher pair, based on interactions with students in the forty minutes preceding the recommended stopping point. In this way we hoped to balance the richness and variance of brainstorming by the full staff with the flexibility and responsiveness of the dyads.

Our collective plans were also intended to help us address students' varied needs. Once we had a workable template, references to individuals and groups began to make their way into the plans. For example, midway through Year 1, one afternoon discussion centered on Jeremy, who had been labeled as having attention deficit hyperactivity disorder (ADHD). Jeremy's notebook entries were very short and often incomplete, but he participated regularly during discussions—so frequently, in fact, that his contributions were creating dilemmas during opening meeting for facilitators. He did not always understand teacher questions and sometimes offered answers that were difficult to connect to the objective. Concerns about the negative impact that this appeared to be having on other students' voicing their ideas led us to embed this note in our Day 7 plan: "Do NOT call on Jeremy first! We do not always need to call on him just because he has his hand raised in large group." Not included in the plan but understood by the staff was our resolve to experiment with vetting Jeremy's ideas through one-to-one discussion or notebook review before we invited him to share with everyone else. We encoded similar reminders in other plans about not selecting the same students to ask predetermined questions of our guest presenters and not inviting the same students to display their drafts at the document camera. In all of these cases, our goal was not to squelch eager students but rather to create space for others to contribute, particularly those who needed more wait time. Without such deliberate intervention, it would have been easy for the most confident and verbally facile students to dominate instructional interactions.

In Year 2 we also became more deliberate about planning roles for staff members not assigned to lead program-wide instruction in opening or closing meeting. These roles required staff to gather data about or provide support for individual learners. Such support might involve restating the task more comprehensibly, suggesting a strategy for text generation, or validating a writing attempt. Students designated for such support included but were not limited to English learners and students with disabilities. Our nickname for this role—"putting a body" on a kid—was borrowed from a phrase meant to describe close defense in basketball that was familiar to many of us from years of following the local university's hoops team.

In the beginning such "body" assignments were typically made during afternoon planning with reminders recorded on the whiteboard during morning setup time and then erased before students entered. By Year 3 we began to note these items in the collective plan to ensure they didn't get lost after the erasure. For example, after a team discussion of Caroline's puzzling reluctance to initiate notebook writing across several activities during our first day, we assigned Crystal, who was not an opening meeting facilitator for Day 2, to position herself strategically to gather data about Caroline for staff consideration that afternoon. This job was recorded in the collective plan as "Watch text generation by Caroline (Crystal)." Crystal's subsequent report suggested that Caroline's behavior was not rooted in a lack of writing fluency, as we initially feared, but rather in her sociability. Given how early in the program it was, we addressed this finding subtly, with a seating adjustment.

In other cases our data indicated a need for more overt intervention. The Day 12 plan for Year 2, for example, listed nine students whom the dyads nominated as having "personal narratives that still need attention." To address this situation, each of those students received a narrative-focused teacher conference early in the composing period, and each spent about thirty minutes on that text while their group members continued with digital story research and scripting. When we reviewed the list at the end of the day, most students had made sufficient progress with their narratives to return solely to digital story work, but Kaid, an

Arabic speaker from Iraq, and Valerie, a Swahili speaker from Kenya, struck us as requiring additional intervention. Consequently, we inserted this note into the collective plan:

Triage to computer room instead of 15-15:
- Kristina—Valerie
- Janice—Kaid

This cryptic note reflected a group decision to assign two teachers who had previously worked well with those students to escort them to the computer lab early, during 15-15. While the move did reduce the students' reading time, we felt it was worth the boost offered by a focused teacher conference to launch a longer, more productive composing period. Over the next two years, we used this same strategy to provide extra composing time for students who needed it because of absences, a lack of clarity about task demands, or distractibility.

Collective plans reduced the planning burden on individual teachers. They engendered confidence and encouraged risk taking, especially when teachers were, as Crystal explained it, "far out of [their] comfort zone" with a focal genre or an instructional routine. One indication of how central the daily plans became to teachers' experience comes from Year 4, when the arrival of hard copies was delayed by an early morning printing snafu. Jake, then a four-year veteran, was rooting through stacks of paper in the LGIR with obvious dismay. When someone asked what was causing him stress, he shared what he was looking for and explained, "I know what we're doing, but the plan is like a binkie," his family's name for a child's pacifier. Despite teachers' familiarity with the plan from the collaborative discussion that yielded it, they found it reassuring to annotate and refer to it during implementation.

Review of Student Work

Collective planning using our shared template was often preceded—and always informed—by review of student work. A desire to ensure ample time for this review was a factor in the generous planning-to-instruction ratio we set and maintained. Those of us involved with the early college initiative hoped that this work would improve the quality of the institute experience for students while strengthening data analysis habits for adults that could enrich academic-year instruction as well.

In Year 1 I constructed a plan for our first review session, scheduled for the afternoon of Day 4, that combined elements from several protocols described in Tina Blythe, David Allen, and Barbara Schieffelin Powell's book, *Looking Together at Student Work*.[9] Under consideration were the on-demand writing samples that students had produced during our first day together, in response to the program's essential questions. (See chapter 3 for more on this topic.) I played the role of the teacher from whose classroom the work originated, Bryan took notes, and Mary kept time and made sure everyone had a chance to speak. The group discussion was structured around three levels of comments—description, interpretation, and evaluation—and we practiced offering a balance of what Blythe and her colleagues call warm feedback, that pointing to strengths, and cool feedback, that indicating potential gaps between the writing and the instructional goals.

The process took about forty-five minutes, and the staff was mostly, though not uniformly, positive about it. Janice liked that we examined the same pieces of work, and Rebecca thought the protocol "helped us focus and stay on target." Nicole, however, described the experience as feeling "ceremonial" at points. Mary shared that it "just ended" and proposed it "needed a space for what one might do"—that is, a component that more clearly invited discussion of instructional implications.

Four days later we tried the process again, this time with multiple work samples—a first-day survey and several notebook entries—from the same student, Nyasia, an African American girl who was a native speaker of English. I explained that I had selected Nyasia because I worried that her quiet, compliant profile might not "draw a lot of attention" from teachers in the institute or school-year classes at Robinson, and I posed "How can we help this kid kick it up another notch?" as a framing question. The discussion that followed was lively and grounded, mostly, in evidence from Nyasia's work, but it veered quickly to consideration of which track she was likely to be assigned in the fall and how successful she would be. The resulting recommendations offered few insights that could be implemented with Nyasia or others who shared her profile within the institute itself. Yet again our attempts at a review process informed by the literature had fallen short.

The process that created more enthusiasm and planning traction for us—and that we employed repeatedly over four years—was simpler than the recommended protocols, and it used tools and processes such as writer's notebooks and whiteboard brainstorming that were familiar from other ways of working together. Although the student samples varied from year to year, they typically included Day 1 surveys, on-demand writing about the essential questions, writer's notebook entries, personal narrative drafts, and digital story artifacts. What did not vary was the sequence of activities:

- Individual staff members read a sampling of student work (e.g., all notebook entries produced on Day 9, as many narrative drafts as possible in twenty minutes) and recorded impressions in their writer's notebooks.
- The full staff described patterns they observed in the work, starting with strengths and then moving to needs for improvement.
- The full staff brainstormed instructional moves to build on student strengths and address at least one need surfacing across the group.

Undergirding that sequence were some principles we discussed explicitly, including the importance of naming strengths before needs to avoid deficit framings and the mandate to ground discussions in the work individuals produced rather than talk of personalities or family histories that could distract us from our own instructional agency.

One powerful example of how reviewing student work with this process and this orientation informed instruction originated in Year 2, although it influenced our work in the next two iterations as well. Our afternoon session on Day 7 that year centered on reviewing student progress with narratives. Dyads brought printed drafts to the meeting, and we devoted about an hour to reading and commenting on them with sticky notes to inform one-to-one conferences the following day. (See chapter 6 for more on conferring.) At the end of the reading period, we each shared our impressions, highlighting notable examples and identifying possible lessons to address needs across the program. Billy recounted revisiting our first-day lesson about sensory details with Aliyah, a US-born African American girl who was writing about an escapade with a friend and an air conditioner. When we compared one of Aliyah's notebook entries with her printed draft, we realized that she had made not one but two very effective revision attempts to her narrative and that she had continued working on her own after conferring with Billy.

We decided to feature this example during the next day's opening meeting for several reasons. By highlighting Aliyah's multiple attempts and the quality of her work, we hoped to inspire other students to persist with revision rather than declaring their narratives "done" prematurely. Accordingly, we inserted slides in the opening meeting PowerPoint presentation for Day 8 that highlighted Aliyah's first, second, and third attempts at particular sections of her text. At the end of the meeting, we showcased Aliyah's work, gave her finger-snap appreciations, and then dismissed the students with a reminder to identify spots in their own drafts where they could attempt similar revisions.

Over the next two years, we used those same examples of Aliyah's revision with new cohorts, but our commitment to continuous improvement led us to slight, but significant, adjustments in our approach. First, we created a handout of the PowerPoint slides, which we sized to fit onto a page in students' notebooks. (See figure 2.6.) This meant that students could use Aliyah's concrete examples of adding sensory detail for reference during ongoing work on their personal narratives, not just on a onetime basis during the lesson in opening meeting. In the collective plan, we also moved discussion of the handout from opening meeting, which sometimes presented challenges in supporting students with language processing issues, to workshop time with the dyads. This shift meant that staff could vary the amounts of time they spent discussing the handout with students, based on need, and it allowed for more precise assessment, given the more intimate group size, of how well individuals were revising. This example demonstrates how instructional ideas and student work often moved across the program's various spaces—opening meeting, team-led workshops, and, especially, afternoon planning sessions—such that each could inform and enhance the others.

Collaborative review of student work supported learning at multiple levels. Students benefited from what Billy called "so many different professional sets of eyes on their work." Staff sometimes saw a piece of work in different ways, offering students more than one viable option for revising. In other cases adult feedback converged, making it more difficult for kids to ignore. Teachers also benefited from considering others' views on the same piece of work. As Jake explained it, differences in perspective offered by staff members who taught different disciplines during the school year often led to rich discussions about writing quality. As staff members sorted through disagreements about how to evaluate student work, they calibrated—and in many cases increased—their expectations of student writers' capabilities.

FIGURE 2.6   Revision process handout

"I'm not a very good writer," somebody once said, "but I'm a pretty good reviser." That sounds like me. I think of revision as "story surgery," a time when I roll up my sleeves and make the dramatic changes necessary to make my words sing to the tune I want.

Ralph Fletcher, *How Writers Work*, p. 69

Revising with the Surgical Eye

Example #1

First Draft: My friend was taller so she gave me a boost. I started taking the air conditioner out.

Revision 1: My friend was taller, so she gave me a boost. She cupped her hands together as we would in cheerleading and I stepped in them as if it was a stool while she lifted me up. I started pulling the air conditioner out of the window.

Revision 2: My friend was taller, so she gave me a boost. She cupped her hands together as we would in cheerleading and I stepped in them as if it was a stool while she lifted me up. It took me a while to get good support because she kept moving. When I finally got steady and was supported she lifted me so I was high enough to reach the window. Then I started pulling the air conditioner out.

Example #2

First Draft: I was electrocuted

Revision 1: All of a sudden I felt a shock go through my body. I was electrocuted!

Revision 2: All of a sudden I felt a shock go through my hands, then through my body. It felt as if someone threw an electric eel at my chest and I caught it. I was electrocuted!

In fact, staff members across all four iterations contended that reviewing work by students with whom multiple teachers had interacted was crucial to a spirit of continuous improvement that defused defensiveness. Several contrasted review within the institute with other experiences that involved examining student work. Nicole, for example, talked about how school-year review of her students' work with colleagues sometimes led to what she called "protective" feelings ("I know he can't write but he's really my boy so don't be too hard on him"). In her view these feelings were muted during the institute because of the shared perspective that participants "were all our kids." Jake echoed Nicole's ideas a year later, arguing that reviewing data and student work from quarterly benchmarks sometimes made Robinson teachers feel targeted, even when colleagues tried to avoid this outcome: "The implication is, if [students are] not getting it, you're not teaching it." In the low-stakes, collaborative environment of the summer program, he felt that there was "no sense of judgment" and, therefore, "none of us had any ego."

Tips and Takeaways

Kristina, a Year 2 staff member, argued that collaborative planning of the kind described in this chapter could be transformative if done over a school year. "Figuring out a way to work that," she said, "would really change the culture, the climate, of everything." To maximize the transformative potential of these collaborative tools and processes, consider the following:

- *Designate a facilitator to document and distribute the group's ideas during both big-picture and daily planning.* Facilitators need not be administrators or outsiders to the school context—the role might rotate among members of a department or team—but they do need to commit to capturing detail and minimizing their personal agendas.
- *Save all documents associated with collaborative planning in a shared space such as Google Drive.* Make sure everyone can access and edit them easily, but take care to archive all versions in case a previous approach serves an emerging need better than the most recent one.
- *Balance attention as a group to big-picture and finer-grained planning.* Too little focus on the latter leaves individuals to figure out implementation complexities with limited support, threatening coherence and increasing burden. Too little focus on the former slows the process down and increases the risk that a group will get mired in daily details without clear consensus about goals and objectives.
- *Use five-to-ten-minute bursts of professional writing to help group members consolidate and share their thinking.* Prompts can be developed

by facilitators or suggested by members. Free writing with no particular prompt can also be used as a problem-solving tool when groups encounter collaborative planning challenges.

- *Review writing samples where student work was supported by multiple teachers.* This practice reduces defensiveness and increases collective responsibility for analysis of patterns. If co-teaching is not feasible, teachers can commit to implementing the same assignment, allowing them to mix examples from multiple classes in the set for group review.

CHAPTER 3

Taking an Inquiry Stance on Writing

It's Day 11 of Year 2, and Billy, today's opening meeting leader, asks students to conclude a warm-up prompt about the status of their digital stories. He then distributes copies of the script for his own multimedia exploration of writing in the professional life of his former college roommate, now a hip-hop musician and comedian. Students are familiar with the digital story from a previous lesson. What's new here is the script—a two-column document with one side for photographs, the other for related narration—that Billy used to plan his product. After the kids peruse his text, he distributes another script for them to read; this one is about writing and the rise of Google, and it was authored in Year 1 by Luka and Marko, a pair of boys who came to the US from Bosnia. Billy asks students to create a new entry in their writer's notebooks for what he calls "noticings" about both exemplars.

In Billy's audience today is Akila, a native speaker of Somali whose family lived in Kenya's sprawling Kakuma refugee camp before coming to the United States. Her warm-up entry discusses the progress she and her partner, Valerie, also an English learner, have made in locating photographs for a digital story about tennis, which Akila plays avidly. Her entry notes two versions of what she labels their "Estentail Questions," one broad ("How does writing connect to tennis?") and the other more focused ("How do coaches use writing to make the players stronger and better?"). Her misspelling of "essential" does not occlude her understanding that their digital story should be framed around a researchable question connected to the program's overarching focus on writing.

After reviewing the two scripts, Akila notes one observation about Billy's text and three more about the Google exemplar. Her entry gains considerably more detail, though, when Billy invites students to make a collective list of ideas cutting across both scripts. Attending closely, Akila records the following in her notebook:

Some Noticings

need sound effects in script

has a little background

short and but has specific details

germatic [dramatic] music to get people's attention

it's planned on a paper for who is going to say what

it's OK for one person to speak a little more than other but no one has to be left aut

focuse on script

need a copy for each person

spoke really clear so others can understand and hear clearly.

The script the girls create over the next two days will have many of the characteristics Akila lists. It will support their construction of a tightly focused digital story communicating information from online research and an email interview with a university tennis coach. In her exit survey, Akila will cite learning "that you have to plan it [a digital story] so you know what you will put in it" as one of her three most important lessons from the program.

This chapter focuses on inquiry as a key driver for the writing institute. I open with this scene because Akila's use of ideas from the lesson depends on several instructional components that are central to our enactment of inquiry. In the first section I describe how our team devised two overarching essential questions, or EQs, that helped the program to cohere and provided varied access points for writers with heterogeneous needs and interests. I explain why we retained the same EQs over four iterations and how we adjusted instructional support to maximize their impact. I then narrow the lens to the digital story and describe the approaches we used to help small groups of students conceptualize and research them under the umbrella of the program-wide EQs. In the second section I describe our use of "noticings," a term we coined to refer to inductive conversations focusing on structure and craft in our focal genres. This section also discusses the exemplar texts we used for noticings, including our selection criteria and our strategies for focusing student attention on text features to improve their own writing.

Why We Embraced Inquiry

George Hillocks argues that one lever in improving students' writing is to frame it as inquiry—driven by students' own questions, informed by their data gathering from original sources, and supported by educative interactions with peers and teachers.[1] Such an orientation contrasts starkly with the fill-in-the blank, overdetermined writing tasks that Arthur Applebee and Judith Langer found to be prevalent in the typically achieving classrooms they studied across multiple subject areas.[2] My collaborators and I sought to interrupt this negative pattern and harness the energy that Hillocks describes by organizing the institute based on student inquiry into two essential questions: *Why write?* and *How can writing affect me and the world?*

At their simplest and most elegant, essential questions guide inquiry by learners into what matters most in the world and in the curriculum. I was introduced to this idea when I worked in two settings—Fenway Middle College High School in Boston, Massachusetts, and Noble High School, in Berwick, Maine—affiliated with the Coalition of Essential Schools. Coalition members embraced common principles, including a preference for depth of study over content coverage and a commitment to all students learning to use their minds well. EQs helped enact these principles, and resources about how to construct and use them circulated widely within the Coalition network.

As my career progressed, and I became more explicitly concerned with designing literacy pedagogies suited for diverse, inclusive classrooms, my appreciation of EQs heightened. Like Joe Onosko and Cheryl Jorgensen, I saw them as indispensable to inclusive unit design, because they helped to ensure intellectual challenge for all learners yet were "tolerant of varied levels of student performance."[3] The best EQs could be answered meaningfully in more than one way and at more than one level while still pointing teachers and students to address common content and skills.

As such, they were a classic example of a pedagogical tool that I have discussed elsewhere as "elastic," one that "stretches to accommodate literacy learners at either end of a developmental continuum, without requiring these students to be labeled or segregated from each other."[4]

Not long after I left the classroom and became a teacher educator, Grant Wiggins, who worked closely with the coalition as a thought partner and researcher, published *Understanding by Design* with his collaborator Jay McTighe. In this influential text, Wiggins and McTighe called for essential questions to drive curriculum design. They argued that EQs should be open-ended, allowing for multiple answers; reward higher order thinking, not just recall; and highlight transferrable ideas within and across disciplines.[5] Before the writing institute was born, the Brown district had reorganized some of its curriculum—most notably, in social studies—around unit-level EQs, and Robinson's principal undertook a school-wide study of the UbD framework during the academic year between the first and second iteration of the writing institute.

These trends meant that most teachers who signed up for the summer staff had a working familiarity with EQs, even if they didn't use them daily. I conjectured that designing and implementing instruction with program-wide EQs would help us address the needs of our deliberately heterogeneous population. It also seemed that collaborative attempts to devise the questions and use them as instructional drivers might support staff members in adopting or refining their use of EQs during the academic year.

Establishing Essential Questions

As I mentioned briefly in chapter 2, the establishment of essential questions took place in the first big-picture planning meeting of Year 1. At that time I proposed that a strong EQ could be "the glue that binds the team" and that a question without a single "right answer" would be "motivating to students." After we reviewed a handout with some hints for constructing such questions and some illustrative examples, we brainstormed the following list:

- Why is it important to write well in today's society? (Rebecca)
- What does great writing look like, and how do I become a great writer? (Rebecca)
- What can I learn about myself from reading and writing? (Sue)

- What is therapeutic about writing? (Nicole)
- What motivates writers? How does writing unite us? (Janice)
- In what ways does writing help me understand my world? (Mary)
- Who do we write for? Ourselves or someone else? (Jake)
- What is the role of writing in my life? (Janice)
- Why write? (Bryan & Sue)

Some options were recorded without comment, while others were discussed in terms of their affordances. A question about the relationship between writing and making money sparked discussion about framing the question to allow students to explore pragmatic purposes for writing, not just expressive ones. When someone contributed "Writing—so what? Who cares?" and read the words aloud with a bit of an attitude, we considered the benefits of permitting skepticism to be explored. We did not want to force students who disliked or struggled with writing to feel obligated to embrace it publicly, even as we hoped that participation in the program might shift those perspectives.

After acknowledging that nearly all of our questions could anchor the program and guide students' construction of digital stories, we tested one that seemed promising. To that end, we brainstormed answers to "Why write?" including:

- to vent
- to woo or attract
- to express
- because we have to
- to remember
- to attract customers
- to attract attention
- to get a job
- to showcase self

As the purposes for writing accumulated, Janice observed approvingly that "Why write?" would facilitate students' generation of their own ideas because it was "so open." She urged us to foreground purposes, though, that were relevant beyond school success. I agreed, adding that I hoped we could link writing and activism. Another team member worried that "Why write?" might be too open and proposed that "How does writing affect me in the world?" might be better.

This exchange led us to adopt both questions in combination. The broader one was intended to cast a wide net for possible angles and topics related to writing, and the narrower one was meant to support students in personalizing and diversifying their writing-related inquiry. Although we revisited this decision annually over three subsequent iterations, we always retained the questions, which we found effective in framing the kind of writing-related inquiry we desired. Over time, however, we did refine some of the approaches we used to help students engage with them, discussed in the next section.

Implementing Essential Questions

We used three primary approaches to help students explore the essential questions in the institute, including EQ-focused writing prompts, an EQ chart, and digital story planning tools.

EQ-Focused Writing Prompts

Students' first opportunity to consider the EQs came on Day 1 when we asked them to write in response to this prompt:

> Why do people write? How does writing affect you and your world? These are questions we will explore together during the Summer Institute. We'd like to read about your thoughts on this topic.
>
> The purpose is to get your ideas down on paper. Don't let spelling and punctuation bog you down.
>
> You will have 5 minutes to use this sheet to do any pre-writing you think will help.
>
> Then your teacher will give you lined paper for your response. You will have 20 minutes to share your ideas.

We had multiple purposes for using the prompt to elicit baseline data. First, we reasoned that it would activate and assess kids' EQ-related prior knowledge. As the instructions indicate, we were indeed curious about their thoughts on this topic. We also expected the writing to yield a snapshot of students' topic development, fluency, and use of details to supplement the limited data we typically had about students' school profiles. Each year, we worked as a team to assign holistic scores of 1–3 to assess the quality of students' compositions, and these scores informed our creation of heterogeneous rosters for dyads.

Despite these benefits, we were wary about the prompt administration creating a test-like feel early in the program. (This was particularly worrisome in a district where many students were aware that poor test scores had prompted state scrutiny and might lead to greater intervention by outsiders.) To interrupt that testing vibe, we included the following in the collective plan, to take place after text generation but before student samples were collected:

> Read-around, with each student selecting a favorite sentence from their EQ-driven writing to share with the whole group; have them underline what they shared with a marker (15 minutes).

In addition to introducing a collaborative element inconsistent with the norms of writing on tests, the read-around made individual kids' ideas about writing—both its purposes and its impact—available to peers and teachers alike. They shared snippets like the following:

- In today's world writing is something that almost everyone knows and does on a daily basis.
- As you keep on writing, you will gain lots of knowledge.
- People write to show who they really are.
- Authors sometimes use poetry to express their feelings because they are able to put it in words and that makes it easier to talk about.
- People could also write to make someone believe what the writer believes. Example: racism.

Across four cohorts, consistent patterns emerged about incoming students' ideas related to the EQs. They saw writing as important. They viewed it as embedded in daily life, although they varied in their ability to support this idea with examples. And the purposes for writing that seemed most familiar to them were self-expression and the achievement of success, defined broadly. The three weeks of instruction that followed this data gathering were intended to build on—and expand—students' emergent ideas.

Our re-administration of the prompt on Day 15 each year offered a chance to evaluate how successful we had been with that expansion. It also allowed us to track growth related to learning objectives such as fluency and topic development. In the first year we were disappointed by the lack of change between the first and second set of samples, joking among ourselves that we might not be able to tell the piles apart if we mislabeled or mixed them up. Many students recapitulated the same set of ideas they presented initially, and neither their word counts nor their use of specific, concrete details and examples increased much. We saw improvements in their personal narratives and digital stories over time, but this didn't seem to translate into more sophisticated responses to the EQs.

To address this pattern, we made several adjustments. We instituted the use of the EQ chart described more fully in the next subsection, which kept the questions more salient on a day-to-day basis. We also added a reflective cue to the instructions for the second administration of the prompt:

> When you write this time, remember all of the things you've learned during the institute that relate to the essential questions, including your work in your writer's notebook, with guest speakers, on personal narratives, and on digital stories. Remember to use specific details and examples, just as you did with your other work over these three weeks.

Finally, we gave students five minutes to browse their notebooks, including the EQ chart, before drafting their responses.

These moves paid off in anchoring students' writing about the EQs in shared, concrete experiences within the program, reducing the number of platitudes we received, and they appeared to support our fluency goals as well. By program's end, 83 percent of the Year 4 cohort increased the total number of words they generated in twenty minutes by an average of 63 words. We saw some of the most significant improvements from students, nearly all of them English learners, who initially received 1 and 1.5 scores on the 3-point scale we used in our baseline ratings. A pattern across this group was a shift from discussing what writing could do in general to a more specific treatment of writing that implicated themselves. For example, Zaynab, a native Swahili speaker originally from Kenya, increased her word count from 112 on Day 1 to 272 on Day 15. Perhaps even more important was the increased level of detail in her language. Her first attempt was comprised of broad sentences with little supporting evidence like these: "Writing can help you be successful in life and make you a better writer. If you want to become a good author or a good writer than you can make that dream come true by learning to write." Three weeks later, her more personalized response drew on examples from a guest presenter and research for her group's digital story:

> I am not that much of a good writer but I am improving by practicing everyday when I am home because I want to do good in my life and become a pediatrician or a nurse to help people. When you are a doctor you write alot because you have to write down what is wrong with the person and what can make that person feel better. . . . And Doctors have to track that down so the next day you come they can ask you do you feel better.

Although writing improvement was harder to capture quantitatively for students whose stronger initial skills yielded higher word counts and better ratings, many demonstrated growth in other ways. A good example was Melissa, a US-born White girl whose Day 1 response to the EQ prompt was the strongest of Year 4. It proposed three discrete purposes for writing ("to inform, to entertain, and to change"), offered specific details, and employed varied sentence constructions. Inquiry within the institute, however, expanded and complicated Melissa's views on writing. Her Day 15 response (see figure 3.1) was just a single word

FIGURE 3.1   Melissa's second EQ response

> I don't think that there are any reasons to write that are more important than all the others. I used to think that all writing could be categorized into a few categories, but now I know that's not the case.
>
> There are near-infinite reasons why we write, and they are all equally important. We might have some reasons to write more often than others, but it's all writing, and it all matters. All reasons to write are important, because all writing pieces are different and they can't be categorized. We write for a career, or we write to relax. Sometimes we do both. We write for school—to teach *or* to learn. We write to tell a story. We write to communicate through letters or email or even texting. We write to change the world. We write because it takes us places. Sometimes, we just write because we have to, and sometimes we write just because we can. They're all valid, and they all matter—and so are the reasons I didn't include because I haven't thought of them yet. Writing is a very personal process, and anyone's reason for writing is unique.
>
> Every reason we write is different. So really, we shouldn't be asking what the three most important reasons to write are—we should be asking "why do *you* write?"

longer than her first attempt, but she broke with the five-paragraph format, discussed her changes in thinking directly, and offered a provocative question in conclusion ("So really, we shouldn't be asking what the three most important reasons to write are—we should be asking "why do *you* write?") rather than the literal restatement of her thesis from Day 1. That she valued her new knowledge and skills was documented in her exit survey, where she shared that she had "learned that not everything should be structured like an essay. . . . (I've been doing standardized tests for way too long.) I learned to feel comfortable writing about my life."

Both examples—Zaynab's and Melissa's—reveal the value of the repeated EQ prompt in fostering students' reflection about their learning relative to the EQs. They also demonstrate its usefulness to us as staff as an assessment tool.

EQ Chart

Another way we structured and documented student inquiry was with the EQ chart. We conceived of this tool after analyzing the disappointing EQ prompt responses from Year 1. Our working hypothesis was that students had not drawn on more institute-related content in their Day 15 responses because exploring the EQs had taken a backseat to completion of the focal genres. To ensure consistent consideration of how participants' ideas about the EQs were evolving, we created the graphic organizer that appears, completed, in figure 3.2. To facilitate its use, we printed it to fit on a page in the writer's notebook, and we distributed tape flags to mark that page for easy reference. We then built opportunities for students to interact with the chart, both orally and in writing, across our plans.

Our most frequent use was associated with visits by guest writers, a program component discussed more fully in chapter 5. After guests departed, staff leading the meeting typically asked students to record connections between the presentations and the EQs. We also asked students to consider such connections when they analyzed exemplar texts such as Billy's script. In these cases we asked students to speculate on why a particular author or group of authors might have constructed the text and what effect it might have on readers or viewers. By using the same tool and procedures for in-person and textual experiences, we hoped to convey that all facets of the institute were intended to help

FIGURE 3.2   Hajna's EQ chart

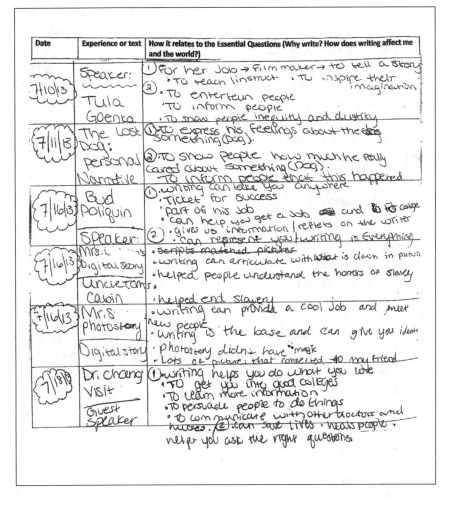

participants construct robust personal answers to the EQs. The goal wasn't just to compose two texts in the focal genres.

As we facilitated students' chart usage over each fifteen-day iteration, we adjusted our approach to reflect our commitment to gradual release of responsibility.[6] During students' initial use of the tool—typically following our first guest's visit—we did not assume that the norms around completion would be self-evident. Following sportswriter Bud Poliquin's talk in Year 3, for example, Janice demonstrated how to complete a row of the chart using ideas from her own writer's notebook, which she projected for students using the document camera. Mary, who was serving as Janice's teaching partner, elicited additional ideas from student volunteers that Janice could shape and elaborate as she recorded them publicly. Janice left her notebook entry on view as a model when she and Mary invited students to add an idea or two of their own to the chart. Each time we revisited the chart to complete another row related to a new guest or text, we gave students a bit more responsibility for shaping and recording their ideas on their own. By the end of the program, this process was automatic for most participants.

Digital Story Planning Tools

Digital story planning tools were a third means for supporting meaning construction related to the EQs. This focal genre allowed students to explore the EQs from angles of personal interest. After several activities to support topic brainstorming, we invited students to submit their top three choices for topics. We used this information to create purposeful groups of two and three during an afternoon planning session (more on this in chapter 7), and then students spent part of Week 2 and most of Week 3 researching their topics and constructing multimedia texts to be screened at the celebration. Figure 3.3 includes a sampling of topics students pursued over the years.

FIGURE 3.3   Sample digital story topics

- Fashion blogging
- Historical origins of writing systems
- Journal writing during the Holocaust
- Lyrics and songwriting
- Spoken-word poetry
- Sportswriting
- Writing in Arabic compared to writing in English
- Writing in various professions (e.g., engineer, physician, television producer, veterinarian, etc.)
- Writing on social media (e.g., Facebook, Instagram, Wattpad, etc.)
- Writing processes used by famous authors and artists (e.g., Alicia Keys, Dr. Seuss, Stephen King, etc.)

In the first year, however, many groups struggled to link topics of interest to the writing-focused EQs. A classic example—to which we kept returning in discussions about how to solve the problem—was a digital story about Kobe Bryant and LeBron James authored by Marvin and Andre, both US-born Black boys. Their story focused on which of the basketball superstars was better but had little to say about how either star used writing to connect with fans or how press coverage fueled the rivalry. Post-program debriefing suggested that the boys' (and other students') resistance to EQ-related revisions was about timing and support. We were asking them to connect to the questions too late in the process, after they had done considerable research that was interesting but not related to writing, and we were offering them feedback on existing text in which they were invested rather than guidance to shape how they constructed that text in the first place.

To address these issues, we made adjustments in Year 2 that foregrounded the EQs earlier in groups' planning processes and created space for our guidance. Most notably, we scheduled back-to-back group meetings before we released students to the computer labs to begin research. In the first meeting we asked students to record their prior knowledge about the topic, thoughts about what they wanted to know, and potential strategies for finding information while staff moved about the room to observe, take notes, and interact as needed. The final column on the planning sheet was headed "How might this topic relate to the essential question(s)?" Students' notes in that column tended not to be well elaborated, but they were revealing nonetheless. If groups couldn't connect to the EQs at all, it cued circulating staff to coach them in refocusing the topic on a writing angle or, in rare cases, encourage them to select another topic.

The second meeting was structured around another group brainstorming sheet. Groups' first, and most time-consuming, task during this meeting was to discuss and record a response to "What question will your digital story answer or address about your topic?" As the groups worked, staff again fanned out to provide feedback on students' proposed questions. Figure 3.4 reproduces an organizer from a basketball-focused group's discussions during Year 2. Their proposed question—"How are the Chicago Bulls talked about by the press (after the game)?"—was already more tightly linked to writing than Marvin and Andre's digital story was the previous year. A conversation with me during their planning generated other sources to consult, as well as more

FIGURE 3.4 Basketball group's graphic organizer

Topic __Basketball__   Group Members' Names __Dayton etc.__

A digital story of 2 to 4 minutes has:

- **Title**
- A written script that connects your topic to one of our Essential Questions with parts for each group member to read
- Approximately 8-12 images (photographs, drawings, graphics, etc.)
- At least one song for background music
- At least one slide with written text
- Credits for information sources, music, and images

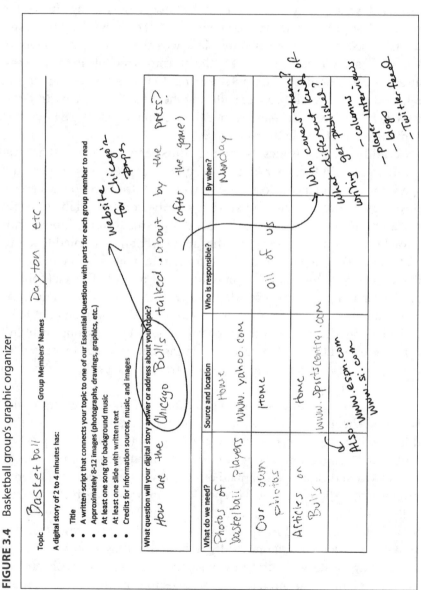

What question will your digital story answer or address about your topic?

How are the (Chicago Bulls) talked about by the press?
(after the game)

↗ website for Chicago papers

What do we need?	Source and location	Who is responsible?	By when?
Photos of basketball players	House www.yahoo.com		Monday
Our own photos	Home	all of us	
Articles on Bulls	Home www.sportscentral.com Also: www.espn.com www.si.com		

Who covers them?
What different kind of writing get published?
 -columns
 -player interviews
 -blogs
 -Twitter feed

questions about who covers the Bulls and in what formats. These additions are recorded on their organizer in my handwriting to ensure that the new ideas—which students offered with a lot of energy and cross-talk—did not get lost for follow-up.

Once students had established their questions, most relied on the internet to conduct their inquiry. They consulted articles from the school's databases, scoured websites, and viewed video clips. Each year a number of groups also accessed information related to the EQs from human interactions. Some of these interactions were connected to program-wide presentations by guest writers (for more, see chapter 5). Hla and Zoya, for example, decided to focus their digital story on the making of the lacrosse-themed film *Crooked Arrows* after a visit from Neal Powless, who served as a coproducer. The girls' script included several quotations from Neal drawn directly from their presentation notes. Other students conducted face-to-face interviews outside of the program. Shelley interviewed her mother, a special education teacher in a local preschool, for her group's digital story about writing instruction for young children with disabilities. A group of three girls traveled together to interview and take pictures of a veterinarian for whom one of them volunteered.

Most students who drew on interviews, however, benefited from teacher mediation in one form or another. Some kids just needed to be connected to a person with expertise. Tisha wrote ten solid questions on her own for my playwright friend, John Cariani, and she worked independently to select and transcribe material from the brief video responses he sent back to her about writing and staging his shows. Clayton, Jermaine, and Winton, who shared an interest in aerospace and computer engineering, needed adult assistance to refine the questions they sent to two professors who had worked with NASA and the US military but no help to incorporate the answers into their script. Akila and Valerie, however, benefited from teacher support at multiple stages of the process, including (1) brainstorming questions for their tennis coach interviewee, (2) crafting a cold-call email to accompany and explain those questions, and (3) sifting through his lengthy response to determine what to include in their storyboard. (See figure 3.5 for the first page.)

Despite the richness of these first-person sources for students' digital stories, we never required their inclusion. Some of the topics students chose did not need such an approach; for example, the three boys who explored Dr. Seuss's writing process two decades after his death had

FIGURE 3.5 Page one of Akila and Valerie's storyboard

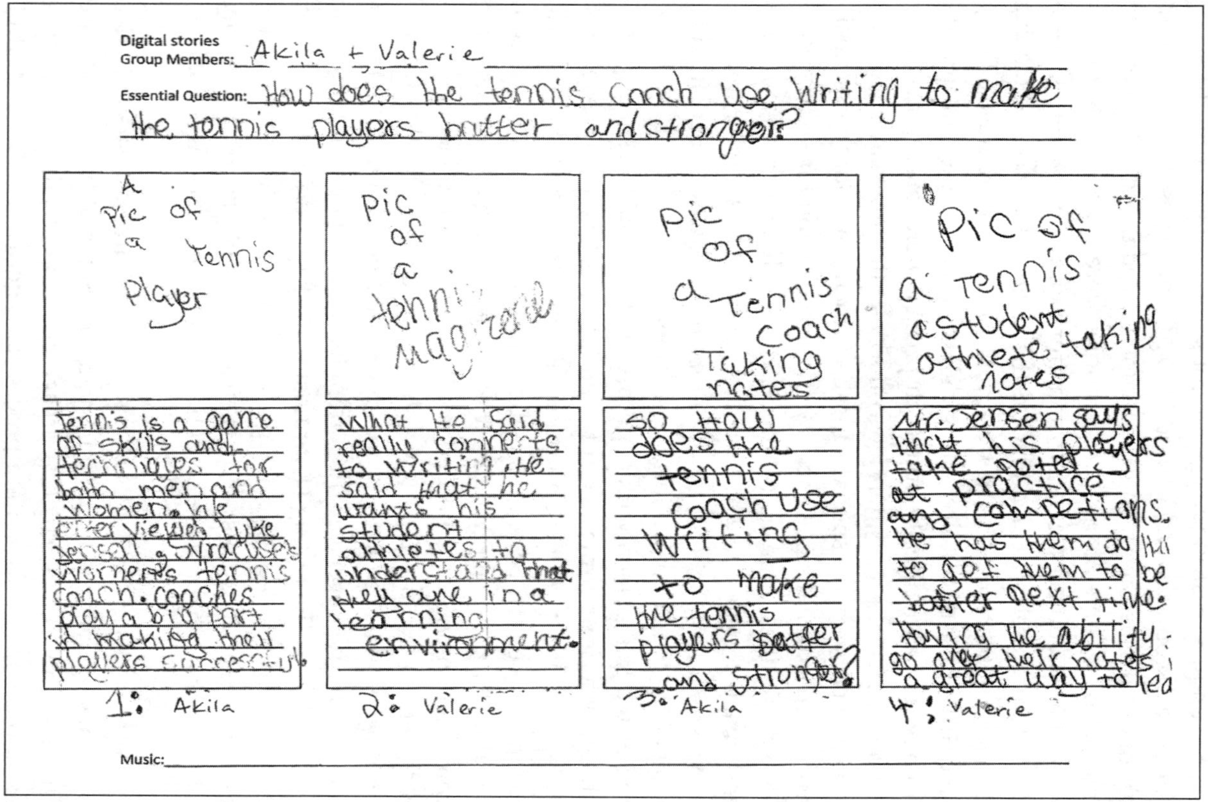

Digital stories
Group Members: Akila + Valerie

Essential Question: How does the tennis coach use writing to make the tennis players better and stronger?

| A Pic of a tennis player | Pic of a tennis magazine | Pic of a tennis coach taking notes | Pic of a tennis student taking athlete notes |

Tennis is a game of skills and techniques for both men and women or experienced like women's tennis coach. Coaches do a big part in making their players successful.

1: Akila

What he said really connects to writing. He said that he wants his student athletes to understand that we are in a learning environment.

2: Valerie

So how does the tennis coach use writing to make the tennis players better and stronger.

3: Akila

Mr. Persen says that his players take notes at practice and competitions. He has them on hi to be even after next time.

knowing he ability to allow helping a great way to lea

4: Valerie

Music:

plenty of rich secondary sources to consult. Individuals who were contacted for interviews sometimes didn't respond at all or did so well after the program had ended—snags that might have grade-related risks for students during the academic year. For this reason, our stance on EQ-related sources was flexible: we invited all students to consider whether interviews were appropriate for their projects, and we provided differentiated support for those who decided they were.

Noticings with Exemplar Texts

A second way we foregrounded inquiry, in addition to the EQs, was with noticings, the instructional approach led by Billy in the opening scene of this chapter. A typical fifteen-day organizer included numerous opportunities for students to identify and share noticings about carefully selected exemplars, what some call mentor texts,[7] in both of our focal genres.

This approach has considerable support in the professional literature on teaching writing, although much of it focuses on the use of print exemplars, such as picture books, with elementary students.[8] Several sources, however, demonstrate the value of inquiry with exemplars, both print and digital, for older learners.[9] *Writing Next*, an influential research summary on teaching writing to adolescents, includes the study of models, defined as "opportunities to read, analyze, and emulate models of good writing," as one of its eleven elements of effective instruction.[10]

For years before the institute, I had noticed a pattern in my work with schools in the region, including in the Brown district. In many of these contexts, writing instruction varied with tracking, whether it was de facto (students were assigned to language arts sections by diagnostic assessment scores) or de jure (students' band participation drove their schedules). The lower the English track, the more prescribed students' writing assignments were and the fewer exemplars they saw. In classes with numerous English learners or students with disabilities, assignments often stipulated how many paragraphs students should write, how many sentences should be in each paragraph, and what information should be in each sentence. Such prescriptions were often justified as temporary scaffolds, but I rarely saw reductions in their use across a school year or a grade-level span. I worried, therefore, that difficulties related to organizing and developing texts in a specific genre reflected opportunity and experience gaps for many students rather than ability differences.

I conjectured that inequitable outcomes for diverse populations might be ameliorated by substituting inquiry with high-quality exemplars for such limiting prescriptions.

During our PD, Robinson teachers and I explored this idea. We used noticings ourselves to explore genres aligned with the district curriculum map, and several teachers led noticing conversations in their classes. The institute represented our first sustained opportunity, however, to test how noticings would work with heterogeneous groups. Over four years every single staff member implemented a noticings routine multiple times, across genres, yielding considerable data for collective review. From this process we learned that two elements were key to successful noticing—selecting suitable exemplar texts that rewarded inquiry and focusing students' attention productively.

Selecting Exemplar Texts

We realized during initial planning that our exemplars needed to help students identify essential features of our focal genres. They also needed to illustrate qualities of effective writing that cut across them, such as language precision. They needed to be high quality and accessible, setting an ambitious but attainable bar for students. And they needed to address interesting and kid-friendly topics, given that participants were choosing, and not required, to attend in the summer.

During Year 1 we selected personal narrative exemplars from three sources: the Teen Ink website, *Chicken Soup for the Teenage Soul*, and school essays authored by juniors and seniors at Robinson. These texts were replaced in subsequent years by strong narratives from past institutes. Staff also shared our own narratives, though we tended to offer excerpts to illustrate aspects of the genre rather than sharing full pieces as we did with student-authored texts.

The scenario was similar, though not identical, with digital story exemplars. No one on our Year 1 team had any digital stories of our own to share, although several of us had read and liked a chapter about digital stories in a book-club text the previous summer.[11] Our exemplars the first year came primarily from two websites: Educational Uses of Storytelling, hosted by the University of Houston, and the Center for Digital Storytelling, now known as StoryCenter.[12] Both sites, but particularly the latter, emphasized narrative, not informational, digital stories, rendering the alignment between them and our envisioned focal products a bit looser than was the case with the personal narratives. In Years 2–4 we addressed this gap by, again, selecting exemplars for noticings that were authored by institute participants as well as by authoring and sharing our own.

As we collected exemplars in both genres, we augmented and refined our selection criteria. (See table 3.1.) With personal narratives we learned to prize brevity, as shorter exemplars left more time for composing and allowed for efficient rereading with a targeted focus. With digital stories we privileged exemplars that clearly represented new learning from research. This consideration emerged after the first two iterations revealed many students' preferences for popular culture–oriented topics such as songwriting. Sometimes such topics yielded generative inquiry— for example, when a Year 3 group interested in R&B artist Alicia Keys encountered a treasure trove of interview and blog material about her creative process. Other times the result was a shallow digital story driven more by images and song clips than by new information. To address this trend, we conducted noticings with texts that drew explicitly on varied source material. Several teachers also selected topics and approaches for their own digital stories that would stretch students' conception of what their research could entail, as Maddie did with a digital story about writing and Civil War–era activism that she constructed and shared during her second year on staff.

Accrued experience with noticings revealed the importance of thinking about exemplars as a set, not as individual texts, to model excellence while maximizing variation. When offered multiple exemplars in the same genre, students were less likely to copy features in their

TABLE 3.1   Selection criteria for exemplars

Personal Narrative	Digital Story	Both
• Short and tightly focused • Includes examples of rich language use	• Shows evidence of equitable contributions by group members • Demonstrates clear connections to program-wide essential questions • Demonstrates evidence of new content learning	• Demonstrates high-quality work accessibly • Offers opportunities to discuss key genre features • Author(s) is representative of key constituency in program (evaluate across body of samples)

own writing and more likely to make inferences about possibilities, reinforcing the inquiry orientation we valued. A diverse group of exemplars authored by peers that participants knew to represent the range of groups in their schools and neighborhoods also presented excellence as attainable by all, not just a privileged few. Our staff conversations about attending to such representation, particularly in Years 3 and 4, helped us to confront unexamined biases and keep expectations high for everyone.

Focusing Students' Attention

Selecting appropriate exemplars was necessary but not sufficient for leveraging the learning potential of noticings. We also needed to focus students' attention on the genre conventions to which they must adhere closely as well as those they might stretch. Our approaches tended to take two forms each year: early on we invited students to share noticings about the focal genre in general; later we asked them to consider exemplars with a narrower lens.

The routine for those initial noticings tended to resemble Billy's lesson from the chapter opening. This work often took place during opening meeting, though it was sometimes scheduled for dyad classrooms as well. Students read or viewed one text in the focal genre, sometimes two, guided by an open-ended prompt such as "What do you notice about digital stories from this text or texts?" If the text was in print, they often annotated it with their thinking while reading. If not, their first use of writing was recording their noticings in a writer's notebook entry. Before launching whole group sharing, teachers typically asked kids to draw a line in their notebook entry under their own ideas in order to distinguish them from ideas generated by the group. This simple move helped students track changes in their thinking, and it preserved valuable assessment data for teachers' review during afternoon planning. Most, though certainly not all, students took notes during the discussion as Akila did in the opening example. The group list was recorded and displayed on a whiteboard, on a piece of chart paper, or in a projected Microsoft Word document, and teachers and students often augmented or edited it in subsequent lessons when they had new ideas about the genre.

After kids began composing their own texts, they explored exemplars for specific purposes. Often this targeted inquiry centered on texts that had been read or viewed before, to promote efficiency as well as flexible thinking. Even then, though, the noticing focus was on students' making varied inferences to inform their own writing rather than transmission of a predetermined teaching point.

Over four years we used numerous exemplars in both focal genres, but our hands-down favorite—the one we used most consistently—was the personal narrative in figure 3.6 that Seth, a native English-speaking

FIGURE 3.6   Seth's personal narrative

For five years, I had a dog. She was the best dog in the world. Her name was Layla. She was really small, she had black and white fur, and she had one blue eye and one black eye. For a long time my family and I thought that she was blind. I wish she was still here.

It was on our way back from Delaware when we lost her. It had been a school vacation. We were on the highway and my dad stopped the car. He got out to change the baby's car seat around, and my brother and I got out to . . . relieve ourselves. So then, my dad and my brother and I all got back into the car and we continued our drive home.

About an hour later, we stopped at a truck stop so my dad could put some gas into the car. When we were all back into the car, I popped the question, "Where's Layla?" From that point on, we all started to panic. Our dog, our little tiny dog, was lost somewhere. We all started to look for her, all around the gas station, asking people if they had seen a little black and white dog. Twenty minutes later we all gave up. After talking amongst ourselves, we all came to a horrible conclusion: If we didn't lose her at the truck stop, we must have left her by the woods on the highway. As soon as my mom said that, my throat got dry and my stomach got real upset. Not my dog, my perfect little Layla. My dad made a u-turn and we started that hour long drive back to the place where we think we lost her.

We didn't go to exactly where we thought we lost her. We all got out and started to call her. Even the baby started to call her. You could hear him in the car, "Yay ya!" It was kind of sad to hear him say her name. It was baby talk, but we all knew what he was saying.

So for another hour we were out, calling Layla up and down the highway. I was hoping she would just pop out of the woods and then we'd all be happy again. My wish never came true. After that hour, my dad said we had to quit and go home because we had school the next day.

That night, no one said anything to each other. I guess we were all just too sad to talk. It's been about three months since we lost Layla. My dad put her all over the internet, hoping someone found her on the highway. That's what we all hoped really, better than her getting eaten out in the wild or something like that. I hope she's okay.

Now three months later, it's like my family just forgot about Layla. They're all just happy like it didn't happen. Or maybe they just moved on. It is over and done with. Maybe moving on would be the best thing to do. Maybe.

Black male student from Year 1, authored about losing the family dog. This concise but evocative piece never failed to interest students, and it sparked many rich observations about personal narratives as a genre during open-ended noticings.

Later we revisited the piece to discuss students' ideas about the author's purpose for writing it. This lesson led naturally into consideration of the program's "Why write?" EQ and set the table for students to articulate what we came to call the "So what," an explicit or implicit articulation of what the piece was intended to convey. Finally, we revisited the piece, which was originally untitled, for a lesson about titles that we started incorporating into the fifteen-day organizer in Year 3, when fine-tuning of our instructional plans freed up time for some additional lessons on the craft of writing.

By Year 4 our team had integrated our approaches such that the noticings process helped students connect the various exemplars—and their own texts—more tightly to the program-wide EQs. This was true even with the personal narratives, which had been more loosely linked to the EQs in previous iterations. Using the same tools and routines across focal genres supported students in making these connections, promoting greater instructional coherence in the program. Inquiry was thus framed as a process to support individuals' varied thinking and composing under a broad curricular umbrella, not the exploration of teacher-determined questions.

Tips and Takeaways

When I interviewed Arlene about serving on the Year 2 staff, she spoke eloquently about how the experience reinforced her already strong commitment to addressing students' varied needs in a dual-enrollment course she taught at Robinson for a local university. In her view, organizing research and writing around an essential question was key for building strong analytical skills for all learners while harnessing the motivational power of topic choice for individuals. As she explained it, the common EQ was the "umbrella that . . . shelters us." As you enact inquiry-focused writing instruction in your own context, consider the following:

- *Brainstorm and refine unit-level essential question(s) as a collaborative process with colleagues.* The multiple perspectives afforded by a group can enhance your ability to construct EQs that will "flex" to accommodate learner diversity.
- *Consider EQs across the arc of a unit.* Adopt a print or digital tool for students to capture their thinking about the question(s) over time, not just at the beginning or the end of the unit.
- *Create anchor charts of EQs and noticings, and display them prominently in instructional spaces.* Revisit and revise these charts as student thinking evolves, and remind students to refer to those resources as they write.
- *Devise a system with colleagues to save student exemplars across cohorts.* This will make a wider range of samples available to each teacher and reduce the collection burden. Online storage via a tool such as Google Drive can facilitate sharing.
- *Name explicit criteria for the exemplars you select, and annotate the samples with explanations of the learning opportunities they offer.* Include information about each writer's profile so that you and your colleagues can consider issues of representation that matter in your teaching context.
- *Practice recording your own noticings about a text in advance of working with students.* You can engage in this process alone, though it's richer and more valuable to do so with at least one other colleague so that you can compare perspectives. When you generate noticings with students, check their list against yours to make sure that they haven't left off key elements you want to highlight.

CHAPTER 4

Using a Writer's Notebook

It's opening meeting on Wednesday, Day 13 of Year 4. Jake, today's co-facilitator, is sharing tips about including music and audio features in the digital stories students are working to complete by Friday's celebration. He instructs them to head a new writer's notebook entry with "Song Choice Workshop," then, harkening back to his college days as a radio DJ, he plays a trio of carefully selected song clips. The first is a slow orchestral arrangement, the second a dance party anthem, and the third Louis Armstrong's classic "What a Wonderful World." After playing each clip twice, Jake asks students to record responses to these questions:

- What does the music make you think of?
- What mood do you think the music evokes?
- What digital story could you imagine it might be used for?

After students conclude their notes (see figure 4.1 for an example from Bethany), Jake invites them to share their impressions. Kids volunteer various moods, from sadness and fear to excitement and calmness, that they think these selections might convey in a digital story. Sue, Jake's teaching partner for the meeting, documents their ideas on the whiteboard. Before everyone moves to the computer labs to begin working, Jake reminds them to talk with their group members about what effects they want to create with the audio features in their own texts.

FIGURE 4.1   Bethany's song choice workshop entry

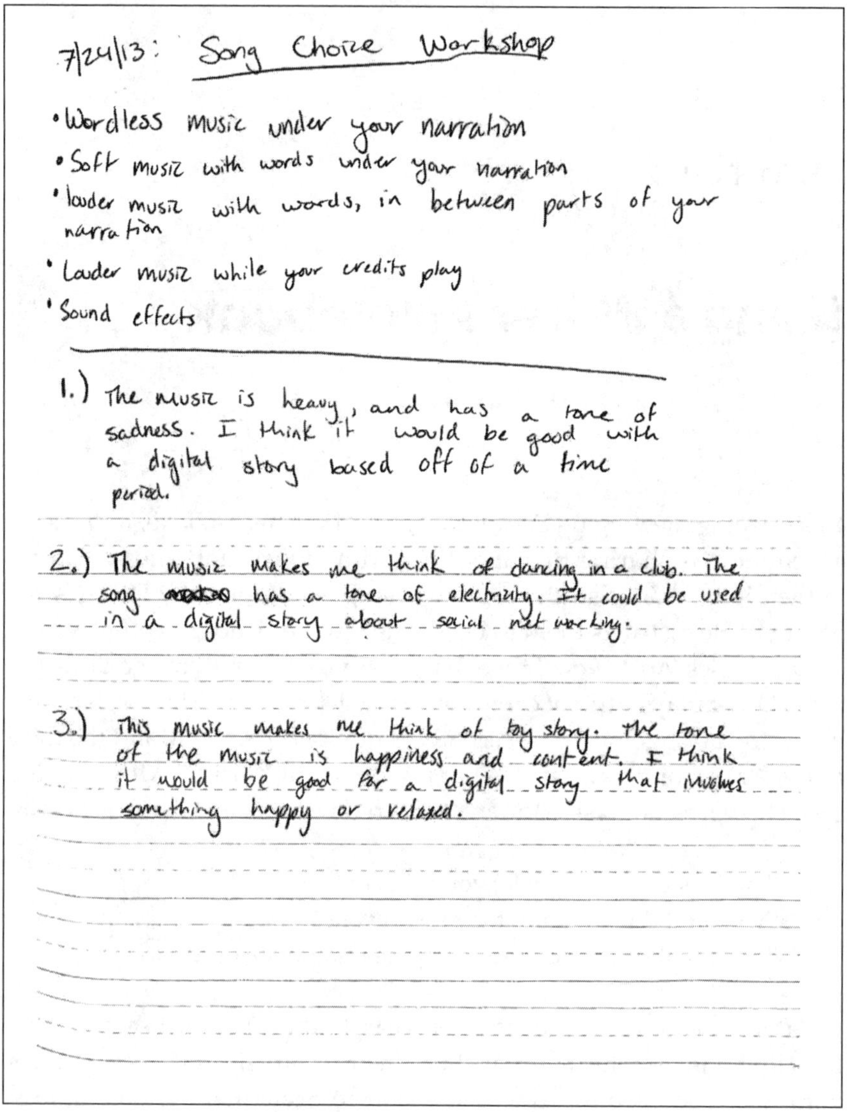

7/24/13: Song Choice Workshop

• Wordless music under your narration
• Soft music with words under your narration
• louder music with words, in between parts of your narration
• Louder music while your credits play
• Sound effects

1.) The music is heavy, and has a tone of sadness. I think it would be good with a digital story based off of a time period.

2.) The music makes me think of dancing in a club. The song has a tone of electricity. It could be used in a digital story about social networking.

3.) This music makes me think of toy story. The tone of the music is happiness and content. I think it would be good for a digital story that involves something happy or relaxed.

Instruction later in the day will focus on several multimodal aspects of composing. In addition to making soundtrack choices guided by Jake and Sue's lesson, students will audiotape the narration from their written scripts, finalize their images, and insert visual organizers such as captions and headers into Photo Story 3. That the day begins with writing using a print-based tool, the writer's notebook, is no accident, however. The notebook is at the heart of the institute, employed daily to foster key dispositions and skills as well as support composition of both focal genres.

This chapter describes our varied uses for the writer's notebook, with emphasis on its accessibility and elasticity—its stretchiness, so to speak—for a heterogeneous population. The chapter is divided into three sections. In the first part I describe why and how our instructional team launched the writer's notebook, setting routines and expectations while forging relationships with individual students. The second part discusses the role of the notebook in topic selection and idea generation. The third part addresses how notebooks supported students' reflection and goal setting, making their perspectives on their own growth and development accessible to multiple adults working with them simultaneously.

Why We Embraced Notebooks

Writer's notebooks have featured in the professional literature on writing instruction for more than three decades now. Interest in their use was sparked for many teachers by reports of professional authors' practice by process-writing pioneer Donald Murray. Other scholars, many connected with the Teachers College Reading and Writing Project directed by Lucy Calkins, elaborated on the classroom affordances of notebooks, with a focus on narrative genres in the elementary grades.[1] More recently, practitioners such as Aimee Buckner and Penny Kittle have offered vivid, contextualized portraits of writer's workshops where notebooks support students' learning to generate ideas, organize their thinking to address varied genre conventions, and control aspects of craft.[2] Although few empirical studies focus discretely on the impact of writer's notebooks, it seems reasonable that their use can support practices such as the development of writing strategies and study of writing models for which the research base is more robust.[3]

Notebooks came up in early institute planning because team members knew them from other contexts. Several Robinson teachers reported using notebooks off and on in their academic-year teaching as well as for personal purposes such as songwriting. Bryan Crandall was never without a notebook of his own representing a hybrid of journal, sketchbook, and scrapbook. I employed them in several literacy education graduate classes, including one where students carried out a semester-long inquiry project. Our discussion of these varied experiences led us to decide that both kids and adults would keep notebooks, so we bought the same marbled-cover composition books for everyone in the program. We built at least two daily opportunities, usually more, for notebook use into our fifteen-day organizer for students and at least one opportunity, as described in chapter 2, into each afternoon session for staff.

Because we intended to deliver instruction in multiple spaces, including the LGIR, classrooms, and computer labs, we did not have storage for handouts or other materials offered by desks, cupboards, or even crates with hanging files. Thus we decided that writer's notebooks would be the repository for all student work not saved on their personal hard drives on the district internet server. Depending on the document's size, students either taped it onto a new page or clipped a folded version to their back cover, ensuring easy access and creating a look and feel resembling the commonplace books of the nineteenth century documented by Dennis Sumara.[4]

Although many scholars make a compelling argument that students' freedom to take their notebooks back and forth from home to school helps build writing habits, we did not permit this. We worried that it would be disruptive, given the institute's compressed format, if individuals forgot or lost their notebooks—individuals whom our experience suggested would be the very ones who needed consistent writing practice the most. Moreover, our collaborative planning model relied on daily review of student work each afternoon. Consequently, we collected notebooks at the end of each instructional session and encouraged students who wrote between sessions to tape loose pages into their notebooks, which some did.

Launching the Notebooks

We developed several routines for launching the notebooks with students. The most important of these was personalizing and writing about its cover. Each year we divided attendees into groups to rotate through three activities led by different teams of teachers: one focused on personal narratives, one on digital stories, and one on writer's notebooks.

In the notebook rotation, we provided participants with magazines, scissors, scrapbooking embellishments, tape, and glue to create collages for their covers representing important aspects of their identities. This task had two purposes, one philosophical and the other logistical. With the former we wanted to signal to students that their in- and out-of-school lives were consequential to us—that we wanted to know them as multifaceted people. With the latter we wanted a mechanism to make it easier for staff and students themselves to locate one notebook quickly among many. Personalized collages facilitated this process much better than undifferentiated marbled covers.

In the first year, however, notebook personalization was limited by available materials, as the periodicals students mined came mostly from the staff's own magazine subscriptions. Since our team was mostly composed of middle-age, monolingual White women, our hobbies and interests did not mirror those of our diverse youth participants. This mismatch was addressed when Gretchen, Robinson's librarian, thoughtfully set aside a large box of year-end periodical discards for program use. This resource made it much easier for participants to find images reflecting their daily lives.

Across all four iterations, even when the magazines were less varied, most students brought great energy to selecting and arranging images on their cover. In fact, so many clamored for additional time to complete the task thoroughly that for several days we set up a supervised early morning station in the cafeteria, before our official start time, for kids to work on their collages. Informal interactions in this space helped staff build early relationships with students by observing and dialoguing with them about their design choices. These exchanges also helped identify individuals who would consistently need extra time to complete tasks throughout the program.

Once students had a working collage in place, we asked them to compose a notebook entry explaining the images they selected. These entries offered several benefits. Because students were writing about familiar, personal territory, most could generate considerable text, helping to frame the notebooks as unintimidating. Students experienced immediate success, which primed them to take more risks later. Staff could also assess students' writing fluency under favorable conditions, which helped to head off deficit-oriented conceptions of the kids. We mined valuable information about individuals' backgrounds, interests, and goals to inform relationships as well as our selection of focal text exemplars.

The low threshold for success with these initial notebook entries served another important function. Students' comfort with the prompt yielded a broad, diverse pool of volunteers from whom we could select to share covers and accompanying entries at the document camera during a closing meeting, typically on Day 3. We were thus able to establish norms early in the program that student work—including informal or unfinished writing, not just polished final drafts—would be featured publicly and that a mix of kids would be invited to share, not just those who had been high achievers in middle school. By allowing *only* positive feedback on those entries and offering volunteers their choice of playful appreciations such as two snaps or a single clap, we sought to build community and reduce student anxiety about revealing their writing to people they did not yet know well.

Figure 4.2 presents notebook entries about their covers from two girls: Hla, an English learner who immigrated to the United States from

FIGURE 4.2   Writer's notebook cover entries from Hla and Camilla

Hla's thoughts on her cover:
The picture make me happy I like the trees with flower grow on it. is remind me of my first spring that I first move to [city]. It was four year ago and there are alot of colorful butterfly flying around the flower. The flower look pretty

Camilla's thoughts on her cover:
When I first sat down to design my notebook I had the idea to make it all collage like. I put some newspaper comics on the background. I used "Curtus" and "Melvin" because thoes are the ones my Dad used to give me when it was Sunday morning & I visited for the weekend. Now that I live w him again it reminds me of it. I put nicki minaj & marilyn monroe because thoes are my babies! They inspire me the way the dare to be different. I also threw my name, a cute dress, and some lips just to fill in some blanks. On the back I put some pages w perfume on them so my notebook smells good. I also threw on a picture of a model with a colorful dress on. That tells something about me. I LOVE COLORS. I put on $, sandals, and sunglasses because thoes are other things I like too. I think designing our notebook was a good idea. It gives everybody a chance to show who they are & our creative side.

Myanmar via Thailand, and Camilla, a US-born girl who identified as African American. Each cover description represented a different area of emphasis for the creator, with Hla devoting most of her attention to the visual aspects and Camilla concentrating more on the verbal. Each approach had value given the multimodal emphasis of the institute more broadly and the notebooks more specifically.

Once students personalized their notebooks, we introduced a number of recurring notebook features aligned with program objectives. These features included several already described in chapter 3, such as students' jottings about their noticings and the chart they used to record their emerging ideas related to the essential questions. Another recurring element tracked student progress during 15-15, the fifteen minutes we devoted to snack and independent reading during each of the program's fifteen days. Students taped their reading logs into the inside back cover of the notebooks. (See figure 4.3 for an example from Myisha.) The logs allowed us to monitor students' reading rates and commitment levels to particular texts at a glance. We could also scan the notebook for connections students made, often on sticky notes, between their 15-15 books and lessons about the focal genres—for instance, by noting the kinds of openings their authors used or by sketching images they might select if their book was converted into a digital story.

Finally, beginning in Year 3 we had students keep a list of definitions for terms such as "documentary," "activist," "narration," and "metacognitive" that surfaced as word-learning possibilities. Kids logged this vocabulary on the last page of their notebooks, where it could be quickly and easily located. Figure 4.4 captures an example from Bashiir, a male English learner originally from Somalia, for "annotate." This term was introduced in a lesson about actively reading exemplars before noticings discussions, and Bashiir used a sketched image in the "Example/ Hint" column to accompany his definition. He also circled *ejemplificar* and wrote in "Spanish" next to that word in the model line we provided in the table. Both moves suggest his understanding of our directions that students should use all available resources to support vocabulary learning, not just print text in English.

These recurring features were intended to position the writer's notebook as a tool with multiple facets. Learning to use each feature was a structured, often step-by-step process to ensure access and understanding for a heterogeneous group. But even with these common expectations,

FIGURE 4.3   Myisha's 15-15 reading log

Reading Log

Date	Title	Page Started	Page Ended	# of Pages Read	Minutes Read
7-9-12	we were here	54	73	19	15
7-10-12	we were here	73	89	16	15
7-11-12	we were here	89	103	15	15
7-12-12	we were here	109	125	16	15
7-16-12	we were here	142	158	16	15
7-17-12	we were here	177	190	13	15
7-19-12	we were here	199	206	7	?
7-20-12	we were here	218	242	24	15
7-24-12	living dead girl	56	71	15	15
7-25-12	kiss me, kill me	3	20	17	15
7-27-12	kiss me, kill me	21			15

FIGURE 4.4   Bashiir's vocabulary log entry

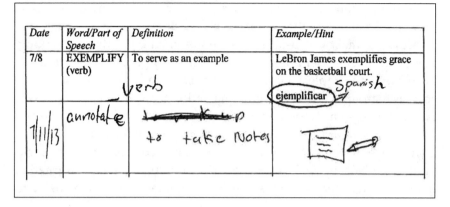

students like Bashiir brought their own sensibilities and approaches to their notebooks, ensuring that the insides were as varied as their decorated covers.

Topic Selection and Idea Generation

One main use for the writer's notebook was supporting students' topic selection and idea generation for the focal genres. With both products we assumed that finding a motivating and manageable topic would be critical to students' willingness to engage in extended revision. We also assumed that many would need instructional support to identify and develop such topics with details in both narrative and informational genres, given the district's emphasis in recent years on writing about literature to align with state test expectations.

To ease students into constructing final products that a fair number found intimidating, we designed what we called notebook warm-ups. Often, though not always, undertaken first thing during opening meeting, these prompts were intended to capture their initial thinking so that their ideas could be shared with others or incorporated later into more extended pieces of writing. Some warm-ups helped students consider topics; others supported brainstorming of details to develop ideas. One such prompt that focused on the digital story asked students to write about three topics that interested them after reviewing a web-style graphic organizer of past digital stories grouped by writing purpose.

Another prompt had students sketching a central image from their emerging personal narratives and then describing the image in words they could transfer to their drafts if they desired.

Although most warm-up entries represented individuals' thinking, there were a few exceptions. Before digital story groups began research in Year 4, for example, we asked them to share and record prior knowledge as a group on their chosen topic. Individuals were responsible for taking their own notes, but what they captured could originate with any member. (See figure 4.5 for an example from a group focused on the writing practices of veterinarians.) This process helped consolidate the background students needed to ask good questions, making that information more accessible across groups with varying interest in and exposure to

FIGURE 4.5 Topic brainstorming for digital story

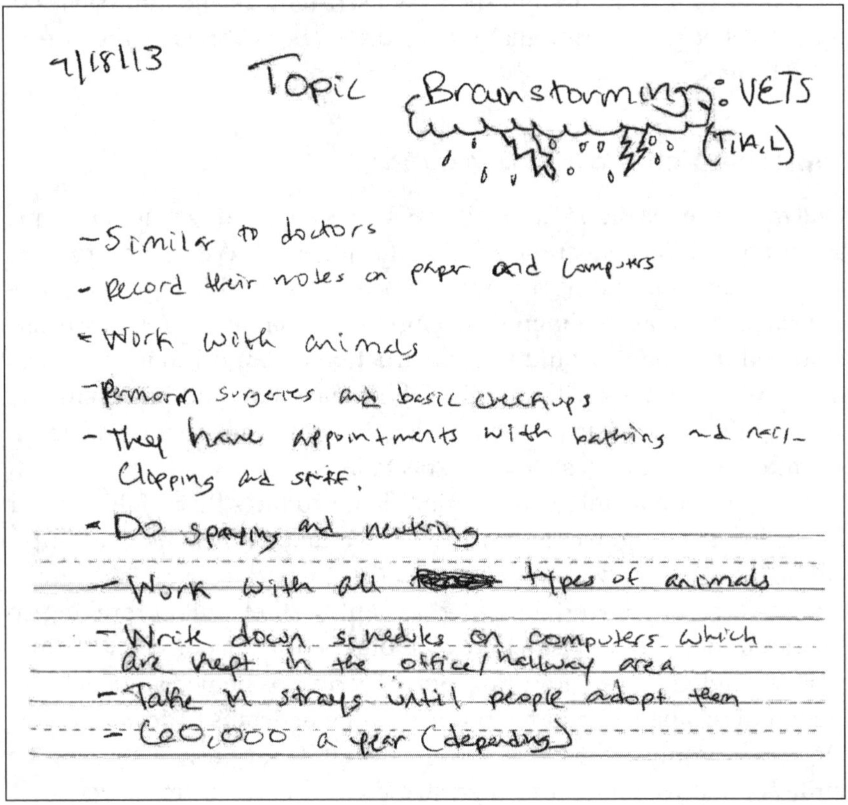
9/18/13

Topic Brainstorming: VETS (Tia, L)

- Similar to doctors
- Record their notes on paper and computers
- Work with animals
- Perform surgeries and basic checkups
- They have appointments with bathing and nail-clipping and stuff.
- Do spaying and neutering
- Work with all types of animals
- Write down schedules on computers which are kept in the office/hallway area
- Take in strays until people adopt them
- 60,000 a year (depending)

the topic. Students referred to their entries when they worked with the EQ-focused graphic organizers described in chapter 3 as well as when they drafted their scripts and storyboards. The collective brainstorming helped to reinforce the collaborative imperative of the digital stories, in contrast to the individually authored personal narratives.

Our most structured and sustained approaches to orchestrating topic selection followed by idea generation, however, had their roots in a text read by the Robinson book club—more specifically in a chapter by Gretchen Bernabei about a protocol called "deciding what to say."[5] Rebecca and Sue had used the protocol to help seniors with college essays. Both thought it could work well to establish narrative topics in the institute, and they volunteered during a Year 1 planning meeting to lead an opening meeting to test this theory. After explaining that the purpose of the lesson was to generate multiple angles on possible topics, they asked students to number a clean page in their notebooks down the side, 1–12. They then guided students through response to the following prompts:

- For numbers 1, 2, and 3, write down words or phrases that remind you of moments in your life when you were proud of someone.
- For number 4, write a memory involving an animal (someone's pet or a wild one).
- For numbers 5, 6, and 7, write down moments in your life when you had to struggle in some way.
- For number 8, write a memory involving a gift you gave.
- For numbers 9, 10, and 11, list memories different from the first eight that you'd like to keep if robots were erasing your memory tomorrow.
- For number 12, write a memory involving writing, your own or someone else's.

This lesson became a fixture in the program, with just a few minor adjustments. One tweak involved taking better advantage of our co-teaching model: we systematized the practice of having one teacher lead the activity verbally while another modeled constructing her own notebook entry under the document camera or on a whiteboard visible to all. This visual support was particularly useful to students who were newer to English or who had less experience with multistep directions because of limited or interrupted formal education.

Another tweak involved how students narrowed their choices. In Year 1 Rebecca and Sue simply asked students to put stars by three of the twelve items that struck them as promising and then free-write about one of them—a choice consistent with Bernabei's recommendations. This approach typically generated text in which students were invested, but we came to wonder whether it supported the decision-making process explicitly enough, particularly for less skilled or less experienced writers.

Eventually we added a component for dyads to implement later in the classrooms. One teacher from each team modeled with her own notebook how to select an option, using these questions:

- Are you interested in writing about this topic, and would other people be interested in it?
- Do you know/remember enough details about the topic to write a complete narrative?
- Will you be comfortable sharing a narrative on this topic with other people?

The first question encouraged students to think about an audience for their composing beyond themselves. It also sometimes prompted useful self-reflection about whether a previously explored topic had been exhausted or not. The second question helped to prevent students from pursuing topics from their early lives that were part of family lore but about which they had shallow personal reservoirs of memory. (This was particularly problematic for lessons focused on elaborating ideas with details.) Finally, the third question helped to ensure that students' topic choices would not isolate them from the institute community. While it is often valuable for individual students to realize the healing that can be associated with confronting a painful experience in writing, a topic they resisted sharing with peers undermined the socially oriented lessons on revision in the fifteen-day organizer. Our analysis revealed that topics with "yes" in the columns for all three questions offered students the best opportunities to achieve our learning objectives. (See figure 4.6 for an example from Malik.)

In Year 3 we made another key adjustment, adapting Bernabei's protocol for application to our other focal genre, the digital story. As discussed earlier, it was challenging in our first two iterations for students

FIGURE 4.6 Malik's "Deciding What to Say" notes

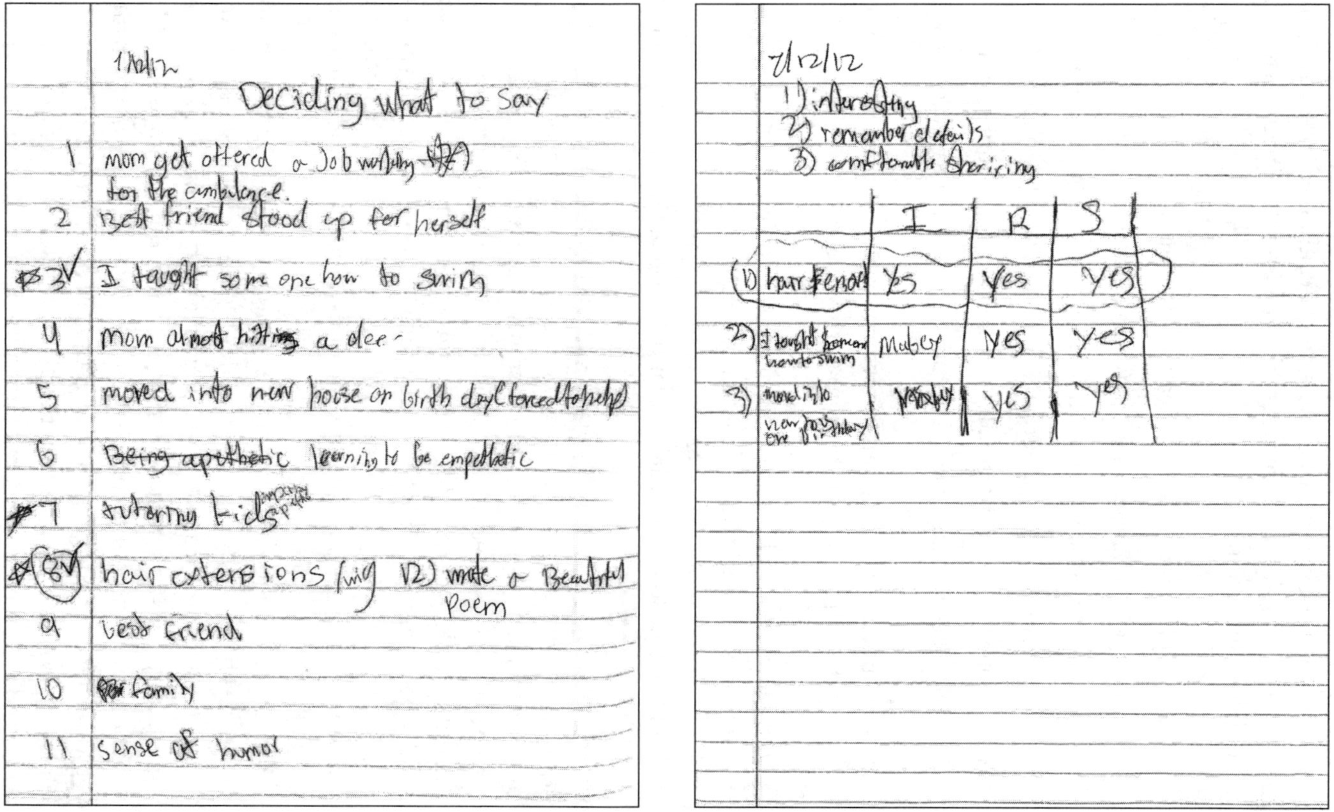

to devise inquiry topics that related squarely to writing. Combined with more focus on the essential questions, the "deciding what to say" protocol improved this situation considerably, yielding student brainstorming along these dimensions:

1, 2, and 3: professions that involve writing that interest you

4, 5, and 6: genres (kinds, types) of writing that interest you

7 and 8: places you're interested in where you see a lot of writing

9 and 10: famous writers about whom you'd like to learn more

11: someone you know personally to whom writing is important

12: a time when writing changed history or some other aspect of the world

Once students had recorded all twelve items, we guided them through the use of the following questions to narrow their lists:

- Am I interested in learning more about this topic?
- Do I think the topic will be interesting to others?
- Will I be able to find information about the topic?
- Will I be able to find pictures and music to go along with this topic?

We advised students that the topics receiving the largest number of starred/yes answers were usually the most promising avenues for digital stories. When, at the end of the activity, we gave them an index card to record their top three choices, most followed this advice. On occasion students would opt for a topic with fewer yes answers than another, usually because of greater personal interest, and we typically validated that choice. The intent of the heuristic, after all, was not to enforce use of a procedure with fidelity but instead to support thoughtful identification of topics.

Our employment of the deciding what to say protocol across the focal genres was meant to develop and reinforce generalizable skills. We knew that topic selection was key to students' ability to produce satisfying, high-quality texts in a compressed time frame. But our goals would not have been met if students composed impressive products in the institute yet were no better equipped to navigate topic selection when they left us. Personal narratives and informational digital stories have different purposes and different genre conventions, to be sure, but by adapting and reusing the brainstorming routine across them, we sought to convey that many writing strategies can be portable when used flexibly, particularly with the support of a tool such as the notebook that cuts across tasks.

Reflection and Goal Setting

In addition to helping students select topics and generate ideas, the writer's notebook served important functions related to reflection and goal setting. We were aware that writing in school was strongly associated for many students with demonstrating certain kinds of competence to achieve a grade from a teacher. To complicate this notion, we designed notebook prompts and activities to help students take greater ownership over their learning—to decide for themselves how well they were progressing and what they needed to do next.

One reflective use of the notebook was grounded in a fluency objective. For some students, particularly those new to English and those with written language disabilities, generating written text was laborious and intimidating. We wanted those learners to develop confidence in their capability to capture initial ideas to revisit for precision later. Other participants demonstrated better technical skills and constructed longer, more detailed texts, but a steady diet of state test-aligned assignments and grade concerns appeared to have undermined their distinctive writerly voices. We wanted those students to focus on their own purposes for writing, not on earning the approval of adult gatekeepers. With both groups we emphasized the importance of developing habits and routines to make text generation more fluid. We compared that process explicitly to physical exercise, drawing on an argument that Jake, a blogger and an aspiring novelist, made about writers needing to "build muscle" through regular practice. We framed the writer's notebook as a space where students could work toward achieving that goal.

Word counts of notebook entries were one simple but powerful way we helped students of all skill levels track increasing fluency. Our thinking was influenced by several studies documenting gains for heterogeneous populations when students monitored the number of words they generated over successive composing periods.[6] Within the institute, we chose open-ended, accessible prompts like the following from Year 3, implemented after "exemplified" was a featured vocabulary word:

> Choose one of the three words you used to describe yourself on the opening-day survey, think about a situation where you *exemplified* the

word you chose, then challenge yourself to write as many words about that situation as you can, without stopping.

We typically asked students to write for five minutes at a time, sometimes increasing to ten, and then to count and record the words they produced. Kids were often surprised by how many words they could generate in a short time when they set aside, at least temporarily, worrying about whether the words were the "right" ones. Many found themselves less daunted by undertaking a 750-word essay or a multipage script when they realized these tasks could be chunked into smaller writing bursts in their notebooks.

On some occasions we had students continue writing on the same topic for another five-minute period before counting their words again. We then had students raise their hands to tally the comparison data in three categories: (1) first total was higher than the second, (2) first and second totals were equal, and (3) second total was higher than the first. Each year the third category was the largest. When we asked students to speculate about this pattern, they made astute observations about the usefulness of getting warmed up and about ideas sparking other ideas. But there were always students who proposed valid explanations for reduced totals as well. A few kids in each cohort reported brainstorming a lot of ideas in the first period before beginning to communicate more precisely—yielding fewer but better-chosen words—in the second. This contrast gave us a chance to discuss the idea that writing production can vary for good reasons from sitting to sitting.

In addition to word counts, students also tracked page counts in their notebooks as another marker of writing fluency as well as of their engagement in program activities. During the closing meeting at the end of Week 1, for instance, we asked the kids to address these questions:

1. How many pages have you written in your writer's notebook?
2. How do you feel about your progress on your personal narrative so far?
3. What is the most important thing you learned this week in the writing institute? Why?

See figure 4.7 for an example from Carina.

When students finished responding, we asked them to "Stand up if you generated at least ____ pages in your notebook this week," with

FIGURE 4.7 Carina's Week 1 reflection

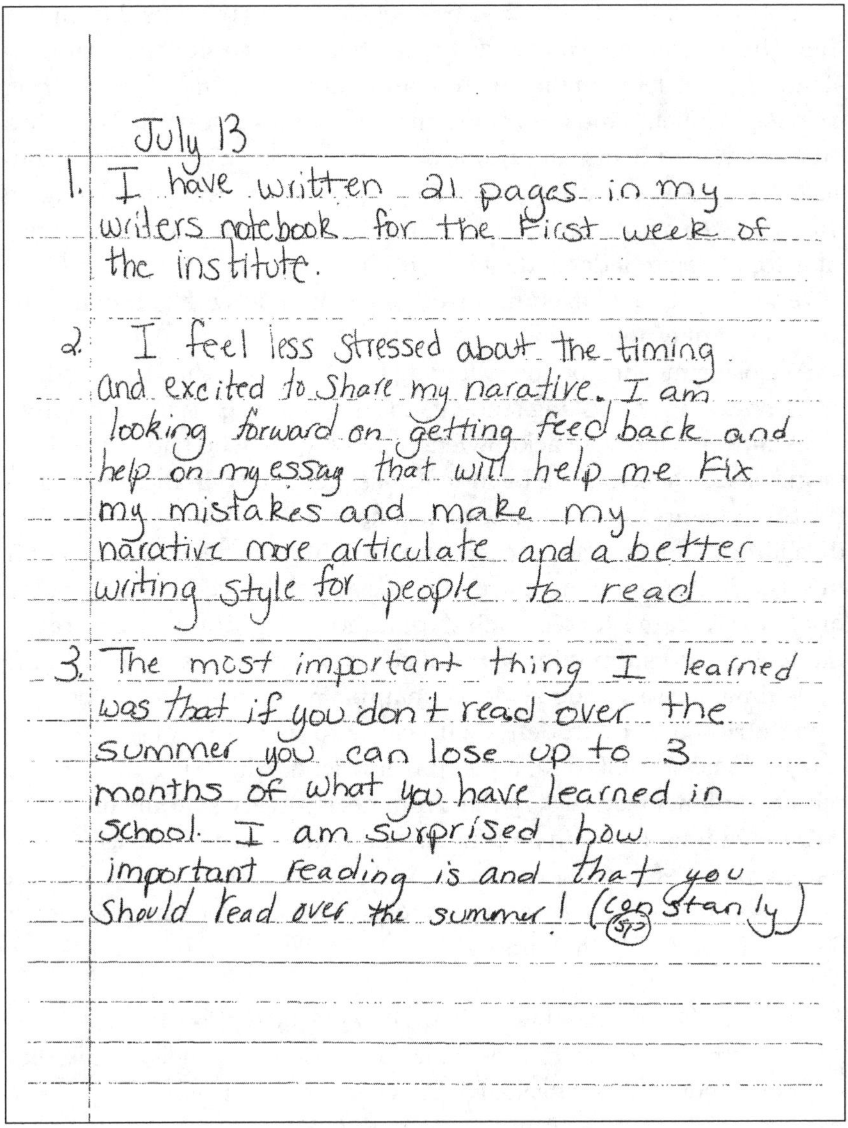

July 13

1. I have written 21 pages in my writers notebook for the first week of the institute.

2. I feel less stressed about the timing and excited to share my narrative. I am looking forward on getting feedback and help on my essay that will help me fix my mistakes and make my narrative more articulate and a better writing style for people to read

3. The most important thing I learned was that if you don't read over the summer you can lose up to 3 months of what you have learned in school. I am surprised how important reading is and that you should read over the summer! (con Stanly)

subsequent prompts directing students to remain standing if they had achieved increasingly higher page totals. Having reviewed the notebooks during planning the previous day, we chose the first few page thresholds to make sure the week ended on a positive note, with everyone standing for the first few rounds before individuals began to sit.

A deliberately generous definition of what counted as a page—including notes, lists, sketches, and so on—leveled the playing field even further. The exercise typically ended when two or three students were still standing, in order to minimize the competitive discourse of recognizing a single "winner." And our congratulations to those individuals focused on outcomes students could control in subsequent weeks, such as consistent attendance or careful recording of text from group debriefing. In this way we sought to highlight that fluency development was accessible for all and not dependent on variables associated with what Carol Dweck has called a "fixed mindset," such as writing talent, that some kids might question having.[7]

At closing meeting on the following two Fridays, we underscored the growth message by asking students to compare their page counts from week to week and then acknowledging everyone who had maintained or increased their totals. The individuals recognized in these meetings routinely represented a mix of learners, including students with disabilities and English learners, who might have been overlooked if the criteria focused more narrowly on teachers' perceptions of writing quality. We came to see such expanded recognition as central to motivating and supporting less skilled or experienced students. At the same time, we saw little evidence that this more inclusive philosophy was detrimental to students who came to us with well-developed conventional skills. For example, Jilly's notebook in Year 2 was littered with complimentary sticky notes from nearly every staff member. Her entries were so thorough and thoughtful that we used them as models with two successive cohorts. As her Week 2 reflection revealed, she met our stated page-count expectations for the whole program in just over 50 percent of the allotted time:

- The number of pages I wrote between 7/18 and 7/22 is 19 pages.
- I didn't write as much as last time because I only attended this week 3 times and last time attended 5 times and wrote 27 pages.
- I believe I already achieved the goal of 45 pages.

Rather than resting on her laurels, she just set a new target for herself: "My new goal is to get to 65 pages by next week."

Developing a positive disposition toward revision was another objective facilitated by reflective use of notebooks. Once students had established topics and consolidated their background knowledge, they did most of their composing on a keyboard, using a desktop computer or a laptop from a mobile cart. As their texts gained heft, students often found it difficult to envision and evaluate different revision options. Many balked at deleting or substituting existing text (which they seemed to find more problematic than adding details). Strategically designed notebook entries were useful in coaxing students to see their texts as malleable. Resistance to change often dissipated when kids had a space separate from their current drafts in which to experiment with different approaches.

One revision-oriented notebook activity, for instance, focused on exploring the effects of varied leads for students' personal narratives. The lesson typically took place in an opening meeting midway through Week 2, when most students had a solid draft of a narrative with a beginning, middle, and end but before the majority had done much polishing. Students learned about different ways to begin their narratives—dropping the reader into the middle of a scene, providing background information about the situation, offering direct dialogue from a character, and so forth. They constructed new leads in their notebooks that would fit into at least two different categories and then conferred with a peer about which option would best fit their intentions for the piece. In Year 2, for example, Adah generated the following options for "Aspiration in Atlanta," a narrative about her family's trip to a civil rights–themed event in Georgia:

- "Adah, come on, the cab is here," my mother warned, impatiently.
- I rushed out the door, with my clothes as well as my excitement packed.
- Traveling, I have developed an ambition for this for a while now.

Later, during composing time in the lab, she substituted the first of the leads in her notebook for a less vivid and immediate sentence that had opened her draft to that point. Such a revision was quite common following this lesson, and even those students who maintained their original leads gained experience with a process of generating multiple options for consideration that they might use with future texts.

Other notebook prompts asked students to use writing to take stock of their work so far and establish a plan for moving forward. Each iteration of the program included at least one such goal-setting prompt, if not several, for the focal genres. In Year 3, for example, we asked students to respond to the following sentence starter before a block of composing time: "To finish my personal narrative in the next two days, I need to. . . ." Neva responded with a bulleted list of action items:

- Not get distracted
- Be more detailed
- Explain more
- Create more imagery

In contrast, Carina devoted her entry to elaborating on one item only:

> I feel I need to concentrate on elaborating key events well enough. So the reader has as much information as needed to fully understand the setting and what is actually happening.

Both examples helped the writer to plan her day a bit more precisely while revealing key information about her thinking to staff. Although the entries were brief, they provided a starting point for discussion with students at work.

Because the digital stories were collaboratively authored, we also crafted notebook prompts intended to yield insights about group process. In Year 3 we asked students to respond to this prompt in their notebooks first thing in the morning on Day 14, the last full day of work time before the screenings:

> Make a list in your writer's notebook of what you need to do today to finish your digital story, then write at least a paragraph about how it answers the essential questions, "Why write?" or "How does writing affect the world?"

When groups convened in the computer labs, each member had ideas to contribute toward a collective plan for action. If students seemed at loose ends later in the day, we could refer them back to their entries to make sure they accomplished the tasks they set for themselves.

In Year 4 we situated a reflective entry about digital story progress even earlier in the instructional sequence (at the end of Day 12) and asked more specific questions:

1. What progress has your group made on your digital story so far?
2. What do you need to do tomorrow and Thursday to finish strongly?
3. How do you feel about what you have done?

These questions appeared to spark more honest and self-critical responses than the open-ended prompts had. For example, Dylan was among a trio of boys, all close friends from the same sending school, who had settled on a TV comedy–writing topic. In his entry Dylan confessed that his group had experienced some "small disagreements" requiring them to "meet in the middle," negotiations that had not been readily apparent to staff. His writing alerted us to the group's problem solving to date, which pleased us, while cueing us to track them closely the next day. The resulting observational data revealed that one member of the group felt greater ownership of the topic and was dominating the decisions, making it tough for Dylan to be heard. The heads-up from the notebook entry helped Sue, Jake, and Joanna, the teacher team working most closely with that group, to support their negotiation process with a light touch.

Another example of useful candor about group process came from a reflection by Imani. For her digital story she was partnered with two peers based on a common interest in songwriting. Although all three had come from the same sending middle school, they did not appear to move within the same social circles, and we witnessed some struggle on their part to come to consensus. Imani's notebook entry demonstrated her awareness of these difficulties and the need to address them before time ran out:

1. Me and my group are getting more done than we used to, but I kinda want to get a move on it.
2. We need to be focused and stay on task.
3. I don't feel to good because we should be farther then what we are now. *We need more time on the script so we are satified. I don't wanna rush and come out with a sloppy finish.

Bridget Lawson, a graduate student working with the program that year, read this entry between instructional sessions and responded with a note: "Imani, encourage your group to continue working hard over the next few days and you will have a great digital story!" The chance to reflect, combined with this validation, supported Imani in taking on more leadership, which led to markedly increased productivity for her group.

The last few days of the program found us designing not just reflective prompts but also several checklists for students to tape into their notebooks as guides for decision-making. (See figure 4.8 for an example.) These tools summarized key steps for completing each focal genre and offered suggestions about how students could refine their texts further if they completed the basic requirements with time remaining. The checklists were central to promoting student independence and ownership of their work. They were particularly valuable on the program's penultimate day, when staff needed to focus their attention on ensuring that all groups had working digital stories to screen at the celebration (and thus had less patience for managing the distracting behavior of those who finished early). Students appreciated the variety of options provided in the checklists, several of which revisited tools and activities from earlier in the program, and they liked being able to choose for themselves what would be most beneficial.

In addition to reflections on the focal genres, we typically asked students to employ their notebook on our last day together to identify reading and writing opportunities for the remaining month of summer vacation:

- What three things are you going to read during the rest of the summer? Explain.
- What three things are you going to write during the rest of the summer? Explain.

The prompt was deliberately broad to invite—and thus implicitly endorse—a wide range of possibilities suited to our heterogeneous student population, and it never failed to yield varied responses. In Year

FIGURE 4.8   Digital story checklist

After recording your narration today, do the following:

	Add credits for information sources, music, and images
	Insert music clips and adjust timing and volume
	Add some effects to make it unique (animation, timing, fadeout, etc.)
	Adjust your background and text colors

3, for instance, Neva's ideas about reading represented a mix of genres and purposes, including magazines; *No Boyz Allowed*, by Ni-Ni Simone, a popular author of African American urban fiction for teens; and *The First Part Last*, a novel from Robinson's summer reading list. Myisha articulated a reading plan that was more school-implicated than Neva's, with all three titles required for advanced classes she planned to take. But the writing she envisioned was self-selected and varied:

- My book "Lost and Found"—I hope to complete it by the end of next year
- Letters to my best friends—I like letters more than texts
- Lists—grocery, bucket, to do, names

With this prompt we intended to send one last positive message of expectation for all: of course students would have reading and writing goals for the rest of the summer that deserved recording and sharing— and more than one of each. Despite our awareness that the specifics of these goals would and should vary for individuals, it was important that the last entry in their notebooks presume competence and engagement beyond the institute, just as we had presumed it on Day 1.

Facilitating Notebook Dialogue

Before I conclude this chapter, I need to say a few words about the notebook-focused exchanges that took place between students and staff. Successful use of notebooks in the institute was not just about designing strong prompts, modeling the writing process, or recognizing student efforts publicly. It was also about adults dialoguing with individual students on the page.

To facilitate this personalized process, regardless of what type of entry was under consideration, staff adhered to some common ground rules. First, we used sticky notes to respond rather than writing directly in the notebooks. Students were thus free to move or remove the stickies as they saw fit. Most left our comments in place, but some preferred to store them in one location, such as inside the front cover, or to recycle them after reading. Either approach suggested their ownership of their notebooks, which we valued.

When it came to the content of those notes, our assets-focused, inclusive orientation meant that we started with strengths. We always named something specific that we appreciated about a participant's notebook writing before we made a suggestion or asked a question about something students could improve. Our use of this sequence—and the overall brevity of our responses—helped to keep the exchanges from invoking evaluation discourses that might reduce student motivation to write.

Other aspects of the responses were intended to strengthen relationships with students. We shared information about common interests and experiences and asked genuine questions. The latter often resulted in sustained exchanges on paper between a student and a staff member. For example, after I asked about the origin of some images in her cover collage, Jilly replied, "Yes, I did draw Nicki M. on my front cover and yes I consider myself an artist. In fact yesterday at home during my spare time I drew some stuff. Check it out." This last sentence referred to several visual representations she sketched in response to the essential questions and taped into her notebook. After Janice gently reminded Bashiir to put a date and heading on his notes, he wrote back, "What do you mean." Her response allowed her to praise his proactive behavior and clarify her suggestion:

> Bashiir, Thank you for asking this question. It was smart of you to get an explanation. And I'm glad you're reading my notes. A heading is when you put a title on your notes so you know what you're writing about.

"Ok," he responded and began to head his subsequent entries much more consistently.

To conclude our notes, we signed our names or initials. Identifying ourselves was essential in a program featuring so much co-teaching—we could not expect students to recognize handwriting from more than half a dozen adults without such explicitness—but the signatures also served to personalize the notes, hinting at a dialogue on paper rather than at judgment from a disembodied authority figure.

The signatures also made it clear to other staff members reviewing the notebooks who had said what to students. This helped us to coordinate and reinforce instructional messages across the team, which was valuable for the adolescent participants. It also modeled different ways of responding positively to students while nudging them to grow, which was valuable for the adults. As Kristina explained after Year 2, seeing "how other people commented in writer's notebooks" was "interesting for me" and helped to prevent her from "getting in a rut, saying the same things to kids." The public, collaborative nature of the notebook exchanges thus had benefits on several levels.

Tips and Takeaways

Many teachers reported using writer's notebooks in their classes during the school year more consistently after serving on the institute staff. Cynthia, for instance, argued that she "carried [the notebook] forward" because she could see that students took ownership and pride in their notebooks and valued the accompanying dialogue with teachers. As part of helping her classes launch their notebooks, Cynthia made her own notebook from the summer available for kids "to see and play with . . . and write notes in with post-its." She wanted students to see that she, too, was continuing to develop as a writer—that such development is ever continuous—and to model the benefits of interacting with others based on the entries.

As you facilitate students' notebook keeping in your context, consider the following:

- *Maintain notebooks throughout the school year.* Our staff discussions revealed that in the past many of us launched notebooks that students kept regularly at the beginning of the year but then sporadically, or not at all, as the year progressed. Part of what made notebooks powerful in the institute was students' increasing comfort with the routines around them and their sense of accomplishment as completed pages accrued over time.
- *Organize yourself to display exemplars from students' notebooks at the point of need.* In the institute we rarely distributed photocopies of student work, because it was expensive and took too much time to orchestrate. Instead, we shared samples by projecting them with a document camera or snapping them with a phone camera to insert into a PowerPoint slide.
- *Keep a notebook of your own and complete key entries you assign students.* You can then better judge the complexity of your tasks and allot time more appropriately as well as share your own work to model expectations and processes.

- *Review notebooks on a regular but manageable schedule.* Students do not need daily feedback to maintain momentum. Considering multiple entries in one sitting is more efficient, particularly with many students on your roster, and it can also reveal patterns across the entries that might not be apparent when reading them one by one.
- *Communicate grades for notebook completion elsewhere if you choose to give them at all.* This practice will minimize the evaluation component and help focus students on the writing process, not your judgment of it. Multiple staff members across all cohorts cited the ungraded nature of the notebooks as important to students' willingness to stretch themselves with their work over time.

CHAPTER 5

Modeling and Mentoring Writing

It's the opening meeting for Friday, Day 5 of Year 2, and art educator and artist Dr. James Rolling stands at the front of the LGIR with a pencil drawing of an African American girl, hair in twists, peeping out from behind an American flag. The drawing is the cover for his book *Cinderella Story*,[1] although he has not mentioned that yet. He is asking the audience to consider what the image might mean: "What is the story telling you?" After eliciting and praising ideas from several students, he explains that his work reframes representations of African Americans as part of a tradition that has taken "very ugly" stereotypes and "reinterpreted them in different ways."

A bit later Rolling provides what he calls an "advance peek" of a picture book manuscript that he hopes to place with a publisher soon. He shows the endpapers, the dedication, and bits of text accompanied by pen-and-ink sketches to which he will add color later. His pages spark question after question from the kids. Moriah is curious about what it feels like to write a book; Akila wants to know more about how Rolling's art comes from his life; and Ahanu wonders what art program he attended. When Eric asks, "Is it hard to remake a drawing?," following up on Rolling's sharing of multiple related sketches, Rolling demurs and explains that repeated sketching is like revision in writing: "The next time, [the draft] is a little bit better." During notebook review in afternoon planning, we discover that students have recorded ideas from Rolling about art as a mechanism for combating injustice, about the power of pairing images and words, and about reading and writing as reciprocal processes.

These scenes reflect a key theme that I explore in this chapter—the importance of adults sharing their composing processes and purposes with youth. In the first section I describe how teacher modeling made new skills and habits of mind accessible to students with varied needs. This section makes clear how data-driven adjustments across program iterations capitalized on the affordances of teacher collaboration to make this modeling more varied and more effective. In the second section I describe the program's guest writer component—the feature that brought community members like Dr. Rolling in contact with youth participants—including how mentors were identified, what insights they offered, and how instruction was designed to amplify the presentations' impact. This section demonstrates the value of giving students access to mentors with diverse life experiences who demonstrate how writing is embedded in professions and affinity groups beyond the school walls.

Why We Embraced Modeling and Mentoring

Research on teaching writing indicates clearly that modeling helps students learn to plan, draft, revise, and edit their compositions. Often taking the form of teacher think-alouds, such modeling makes complex tasks more manageable for learners and is a crucial element of the framework of gradually releasing responsibility that we embraced in the institute.[2] Although modeling benefits learners of all profiles, it provides the most powerful boost for low-achieving writers, including those from groups who are traditionally under-served in schools.[3]

Explicit but responsive teacher modeling (as opposed to the delivery of a predetermined instructional script) is less common in American schools than it should be, given the strength of the evidence base.[4] Limited attention to writing during teacher preparation, time pressures associated with crowded curricula, and many teachers' preference for literature study over composition combine to limit access to high-quality modeling for many students. Nonetheless, initiatives such as the National Writing Project (NWP) have established that teachers with an active writing practice can model writerly engagement as well as demystify the demands of particular composing tasks.[5] Well-known English teacher and consultant Kelly Gallagher, himself a participant in the NWP-affiliated South Basin Writing Project, frames his entire book, *Write Like This*, with this view, arguing: "Of all the strategies I have learned over the years, there is one that stands far above the rest when it comes to improving my students' writing: the teacher should model by writing—and think out loud while writing—in front of the class."[6] According to Gallagher, what matters most is not that teachers write *well* in front of their students but that they demonstrate the writing process in all its complexity, including their own false starts, their struggles, and the work-arounds they devise to solve problems.

As delineated in the guidance document I shared in chapter 1, modeling via teacher think-alouds was a practice that Robinson teachers and I explored together during academic-year PD. The summer institute extended that work. Staff members varied in how comfortable they were as writers as well as how much they privileged writing relative to other curricular foci. Some saw modeling as an essential tool for building student writers' capacity. Others, with Jake most vocal among them, worried that too much modeling would limit student creativity and encourage low-level replication of teacher products. These doubts and differences aside, we united to investigate what would happen in the institute when we shifted our instructional framing for writing tasks from "Let me tell you how to do that" to "Let me show you how I do that." We agreed to foreground the demonstration of writing processes over the creation of detailed assignment descriptions or scoring rubrics of the kind that many teachers use during the school year. We hoped that we could design and implement more effective modeling collaboratively than any of us had previously done individually.

Also influencing our thinking about how to address opportunity and achievement gaps for predictable groups of Robinson students was emerging research suggesting that students benefit not only from knowing about the writing histories and accomplishments of people who share their backgrounds but also from direct interactions with writing mentors who look and sound like them.[7] Since most institute staff members were White, monolingual women—a pattern consistent with Robinson's teaching force as well as with American teachers in general[8]—our ability to provide such mentorship directly for our diverse population was constrained. Our shared status as teachers was a limiting factor as well, particularly given a belief among many youth we served that writing was primarily about succeeding in school (an idea we wanted the institute to dislodge).

Collaborating with community members like James Rolling was thus meant to complement teacher modeling and address these limitations. Presentations by guest writers who were not K–12 teachers not only increased the ethnic and linguistic diversity of the mentor pool available to our students; they also offered a wider set of perspectives on our essential questions, particularly when it came to varied purposes and uses for writing. Over time we learned to recruit these guests more deliberately and to leverage their mentoring contributions more powerfully, just as we learned to plan and deliver more effective modeling ourselves.

Modeling

In this section I describe our use of modeling—instructional approaches combining verbal explanation and visual demonstration to make writing processes explicit to learners—within the institute. Most often such modeling involved a teacher thinking aloud while planning, drafting, or revising in front of students, although a variation also involved displaying a series of existing artifacts in sequence while narrating the processes that led to their production. In either case the purpose was the same: to show how an experienced writer facing a specific writing task or problem used insights and routines learners could apply later to their own writing.

Modeling by Individual Teachers

The most frequent instances of modeling in the institute involved individual teacher demonstrations related to one of the two focal genres. These demonstrations typically focused on an aspect of composing that review of student products or past experience suggested would be helpful to most, if not all, participants. Modeling often took place during opening meeting, led by a teacher who volunteered or was nominated for the job during afternoon planning, although we sometimes built it into dyad time instead if we thought students might benefit from the smaller group size.

One example of such individual teacher modeling in Year 1 involved a digital story about my grandmother's use of writing to cope with her dementia, which I linked to memories of her encouraging my journal keeping during summers at our family camp. I led the lesson using a partially completed story that paired chunks of recorded narration with images on various slides but included no music or credits. My modeling focused on the relationship between the narration and the images, a component of multimodal composing that students often saw as simple but that could be deceptively complex.

To support students in less literal thinking about the visual aspects of their stories, I played my draft example and then projected my three-column scripting tool to explain, slide by slide, why I had selected each image and where I had located it. Because my narration drew on family history, current experience, and my research on dementia, I used images from my childhood scrapbooks, my phone camera, and the internet. Some of my pairings were quite straightforward—for example, when I illustrated a description of typical camp activities with an image of my ten-year-old self and my cousin beaming before a string of fresh-caught trout. Others, however, required more explanation, including how I photographed a contemporary journal to represent one lost from childhood and how I searched Google Images with "confusion" as a keyword to locate a piece of abstract art to signify my grandmother's feelings after her diagnosis. I concluded the lesson by reminding students to vary the sources for their own images and inviting them to suggest music they thought would be appropriate, given the tone of my digital story so far.

The next three iterations of the institute featured a good deal of modeling like this, with teachers increasingly taking over the digital story modeling once our May and June planning better supported their construction of their own texts. Although the impact of the modeling was difficult to isolate definitively from the other instructional approaches we employed, our interactions with students, as well as our review of their products, suggest that many of the students adopted our methods. Figure 5.1, for example, reproduces the first page of a draft script, typed by Lina, for her group's digital story focused on the writing practices of veterinarians. The third column of the planning tool includes images from the kinds of internet searches that were typical for students. But it also refers to several photographs that Linda, Gemma, and Janie took when they visited the vet's office in person not long after Billy, back for a second year on staff, modeled the potential of original images with his own digital story. The vet group's work bears the tracks of thinking that Billy made visible with his model. Lina, for example, recorded in her notebook how well "the pictures match the script" and noted that "the pictures changed pretty fast," requiring quite a few to be collected.

FIGURE 5.1   Page one of a draft digital story script

Digital Story Planning Tool

Note: Draw an arrow down if an image or music continues beyond one box.

Narration	Speaker(s)	Image	Music
Veterinarians are doctors that tend to the health of all animals. They diagnose, treat, or research medical conditions and diseases of pets, livestock, and animals across the world. They perform surgeries and vaccinate animals against diseases also.	Janie	All animals and vet with cat medicine	
There are 4 year veterinary medical colleges that are similar to medical schools for doctors. Vets must complete a Doctor of Veterinary Medicine (D.V.M.) and pass the North American Veterinary Licensing Exam to become a vet.	Lina	One pic of a vet exam	
We went to the XXXX Village Veterinary Hospital to interview the owner, a vet, about his job there. We were looking to find out how writing is connected to being a veterinarian.	Gemma	Picture of animal hospital/ Dr. W with dog	
According to Dr. W., vets use writing in their everyday jobs by writing history and diagnostic notes and findings of physical exams of animals.	Janie	Pic of vet writing	
The best part of Dr. W.'s job is making sure the animals are healthy, stay well and live happy lives. The worst part of the job is when you cannot save an animal because they are too old or sick.	Lina	Vet with puppy	
He showed us around the animal hospital and let us watch a surgery in action and see some of the animals being treated or taken in to the hospital.	Gemma	Surgery at animal hospital/ the nurse with two Boston terriers	

This is not to say, however, that teacher modeling always went smoothly. One issue with which we wrestled was our own assumption that effective modeling should be interactive. Many institute staff members, including myself, had read resources and attended professional development sessions that called for eliciting student perspectives and limiting teacher talk in order to increase engagement. A teacher demonstration without student input seemed for some to align with a discredited direct instruction paradigm. What we realized, however, from watching one another lead more and less direct modeling sessions was that eliciting students' ideas during a teacher think-aloud often devolved into a game of "guess what's in the teacher's head." Increasing student participation did not necessarily increase mastery of the learning objective. Sometimes such participation created confusion, particularly if the discussion was dominated by students like Jeremy, the boy profiled in chapter 2 whose thinking often diverged from the lesson focus. In such situations, peer contributions could distract from the main point, making it difficult for students to use content from the lesson in their own subsequent writing.

Over time we learned to offer teacher modeling that was more sharply delineated from the other, more interactive approaches we employed. This evolution in our thinking is best exemplified by changes across several iterations in a lesson on leads for personal narratives. Jake, an accomplished fiction writer in his life outside school, took the lead on this lesson in opening meeting during Years 2–4. Our collective plan called for him to model different types of leads with examples from his own writing before asking students to generate options in those categories for their own narratives. Jake's first delivery of this lesson had numerous strengths: the lead examples were funny and personal, and they illustrated each type clearly. But the lesson ran long (always a risk with a big, heterogeneous group like ours) when Jake invited students to share their impressions between examples—a move that focused numerous kids on gleaning more information about Jake's childhood than on grasping how each lead fit the types we wanted them to consider. As we debriefed lessons like this one that blurred the lines between direct instruction and discussion, we realized how difficult they could be for some students to follow, particularly for students new to English or those identified with oral language–implicated disabilities.

By Year 4 we fine-tuned Jake's lesson to address these concerns while retaining its strong original features. His exemplar leads were still rich and distinct, but now his accompanying language was crisp and clear, with little back-and-forth with students to muddy the message. It took him just six minutes to model the task, well within the attention span of our audience. Once the types were presented, he invited students to vote for their favorites and then explain their choices—a move that introduced a language structure other than teacher talk at the same time it allowed students to practice the kind of thinking we wanted them to do after generating their own lead alternatives. This combination of approaches—a brief burst of uninterrupted teacher talk, carefully planned to illustrate a discrete point in accessible language, followed by teacher-student interaction around how to use that content—emerged as the most effective kind of modeling in our context, and we used it repeatedly, with both focal genres, across our fifteen-day organizers.

Modeling by Multiple Adults in Shared Space

As we refined the institute across iterations, we also learned to make better use of the modeling potential offered by multiple adults working in shared space. We leveraged this collaborative potential in three ways: (1) making teachers' informal writing more visible to learners, (2) combining task instructions with a simultaneous visual demonstration, and (3) demonstrating peer-to-peer interaction around a piece of writing.

To model approaches to informal writing, not just the production of the focal genres, more explicitly, we planned for teachers not assigned to facilitation or student-support roles during opening and closing meetings to complete the same tasks as students. When the adults composed, they demonstrated what writing engagement could look like; when they shared, their products offered new ways of using language to supplement the models provided by those leading the lesson. During Year 4, for example, Sue and Janice co-led a Day 1 activity intended to introduce the writer's notebook as a tool for idea generation.[9] Participants made lists of words associated with writing and then constructed as many three-word sentences or phrases as they could using those words. After Sue and Janice modeled the task using a summer theme that we expected to be readily accessible to students ("Sleeping past six," "Swim all day"), they turned on a timer for three minutes of composing. Our collective plan called for them to "Have a sampling of kids and at least 1 teacher share out loud to full group," and it reminded them that "the teacher shouldn't go first," to establish student voices strongly before introducing those of the adults. After eight youth volunteered contributions such as "The plot thickens" (Bethany), "Always check spelling" (Bashiir), and "Pens leak ink" (John), Crystal, who was returning to the staff for a second year, shared "Fill those pages," with an aspirational tone in her voice that prompted both adolescents and adults to chuckle.

Teacher modeling from a participant stance like Crystal's offered numerous benefits. It presented the tasks as worth doing by adults, not just as school assignments. It positioned the teachers as community members open to vulnerability and growth in the same ways we asked youth to be. It also supported our differentiation efforts. Sometimes staff shared concrete, accessible examples to students who needed them. (Maddie and Janice were particularly inclined to offer such modeling, having honed such skills during their academic-year positions in English as a new language and special education, respectively.) At other times staff contributions were deliberately more sophisticated than what most students could produce, setting the bar high for all learners but with special concern for keeping our most skilled and experienced students on the edge of challenge.

We also began to embed simultaneous teacher demonstration in our direction giving for composing tasks. In Year 3, for example, Jake and Maddie worked together to lead students through the various steps associated with the "deciding what to say" activity described in chapter 4. In previous years, teacher facilitators of this activity had always taken turns in offering instructions and verbal examples, but Jake and Maddie's co-teaching went one step further. Jake took charge of the slides with the various prompts while Maddie responded to those prompts from her own perspective on the whiteboard. (See figure 5.2.) Her concrete, visual model seemed especially helpful to English language learners, who had sometimes struggled with the complexity of the instructions in the past. When we reviewed the entries during afternoon planning that day, veteran staff members like Janice and Mary noticed fewer blank and incomplete responses among the ELLs than in previous iterations. This pattern led us to designate a co-teacher to provide a simultaneous public model for most subsequent lessons including multistep directions.

On still other occasions, pairs of teachers modeled interactive processes we wanted student writers to use with one another to increase the quality of their work. One notable example took place at the end of the first week of Year 4. By then most students had a solid start on their personal narratives. Our experience with previous cohorts suggested,

FIGURE 5.2   Maddie's modeling of digital story topic generation

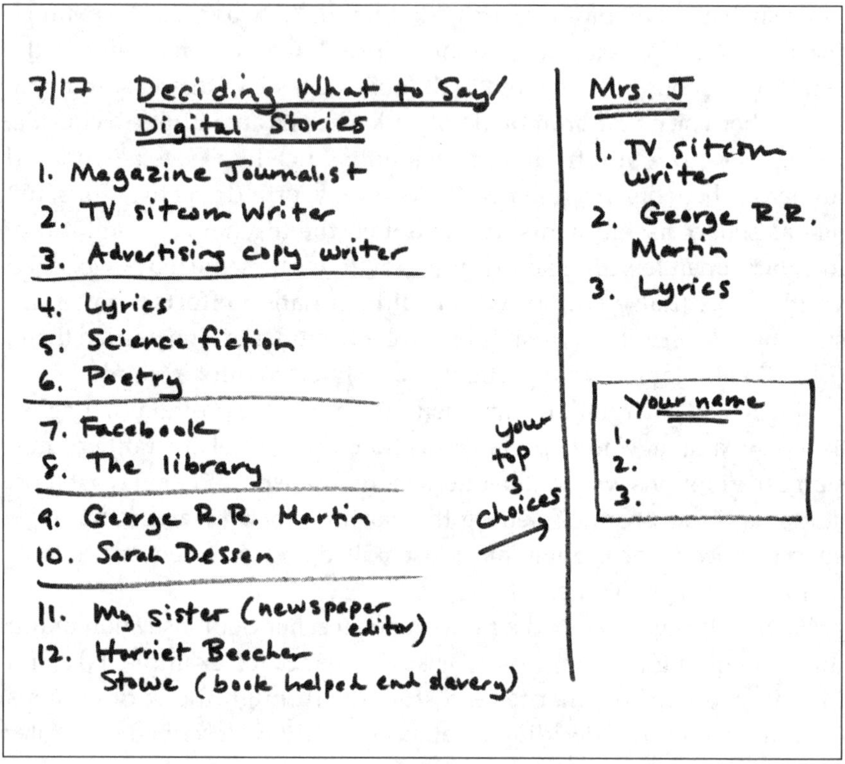

7/17   Deciding What to Say/
        Digital Stories

1. Magazine Journalist
2. TV sitcom Writer
3. Advertising copy writer

4. Lyrics
5. Science fiction
6. Poetry

7. Facebook
8. The library

9. George R.R. Martin
10. Sarah Dessen

11. My sister (newspaper editor)
12. Harriet Beecher
      Stowe (book helped end slavery)

your top 3 choices →

Mrs. J

1. TV sitcom writer
2. George R.R. Martin
3. Lyrics

Your name
1.
2.
3.

though, that many kids would need support to develop their ideas fully and refine their language choices. When we talked during planning about how to provide this support, the group was keen on Janice's suggestion to focus kids' attention on descriptive language. Our review of student work revealed that some students had few descriptive details in their drafts, while others had details that appeared unrelated to the point of their pieces. We thought that both groups might benefit from instruction focused on the impact of well-chosen sensory details on a reader's experience. Concerned about making this idea more concrete, Maddie proposed that we incorporate a visual. Janice and Billy, who were dyad partners that year, began to riff on how to do this, using examples from a narrative about a car accident that Janice had been writing that week and sharing with their dyad group. I recorded notes on the whiteboard from the discussion that we quickly shaped into an outline for the next day's opening meeting.

During that meeting Janice and Billy modeled what we came to label a "joint think-aloud" in our collective plans, with Janice playing the role of writer and Billy that of peer reader. Janice sketched a central image from her narrative—a rudimentary car in motion—and wrote a single sentence to accompany it: "The car went off the road." She then asked Billy to tell her what else he wanted to know about the sentence or the image as a potential reader. He shared half a dozen questions, which Janice recorded so that students could see them. She then wrote a new sentence, publicly, that addressed several of his questions, including whether the car was going fast and where it ended up: "The car flew off the road like a cardinal darting into the trees." She made it clear that she would think about answering Billy's remaining questions in other parts of the narrative—that she would not try to jam all of the answers into a single overloaded sentence. The two of them then co-led a brief discussion of what students noticed about their interaction before asking students to pair up and use the same process with their own narratives.

This joint modeling was revealed as generative when we listened in on the pairs' conversations and, later, reviewed their notebook entries. Kevin, a US-born Black boy, was writing a strikingly funny personal narrative about a prank that his mother had played on him. His sketch and initial sentence, reproduced in figure 5.3, indicated that he did not quite understand Janice and Billy's directions for the task, as he wrote in the third person ("a boy is cry since he is bald") rather than the first-person voice he was using in the narrative itself. His peer exchange with Rachel set him right, however, generating a list of nine questions and some new, narrative-ready text: "On monday at my house my mom shaved my hair bald. When I saw it I was crying. It was so shiny you can see your own reflection on my head." Irregularities in verb tense notwithstanding, that last sentence was a gem—exactly the kind of vivid language we hoped the lesson would promote—and its debt to the star on the boy's head in the drawing was clear.

Sahra, a Somali-born girl who immigrated to the United States via Kenya, had a similarly generative exchange with her partner, Gemma. Sahra's narrative was about receiving a new Barbie doll as a gift from her stepfather, who had moved to the States ahead of the rest of the family. The image in her notebook was a line drawing of a woman in a dress with masses of hair, accompanied by this sentence: "My new Barbie doll was Beautiful." Sahra's exchange with Gemma, who was clearly familiar

FIGURE 5.3 Kevin's notebook entry

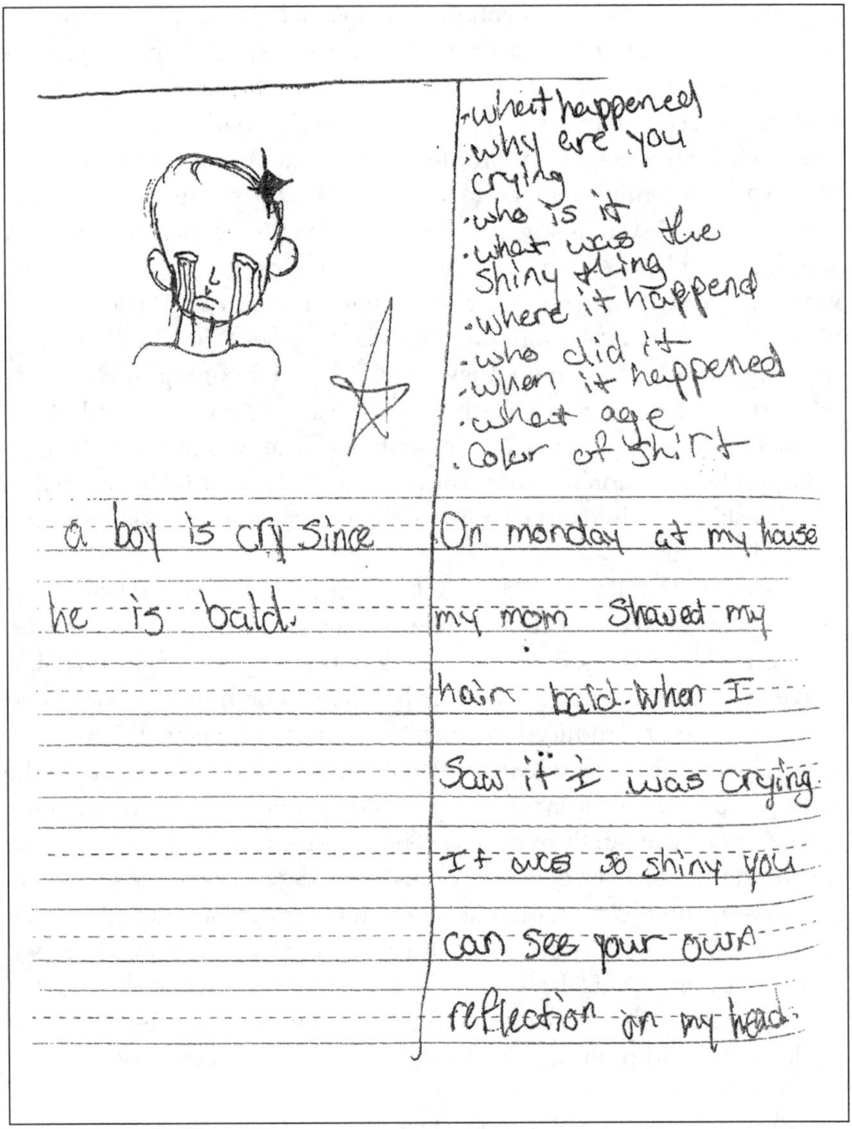

with Barbie and her accoutrements, yielded seven questions, reproduced verbatim below:

- What did she look like?
- What was she wearing?
- What color?
- What style her hair was in?
- Did she have jewelry?
- What type of shoes?
- What accesories she came with?

After the conversation, Sahra wrote a much more detailed description ("My new Barbie doll had on a pink sparkly dress with pink, high heels, and she had curly blond hair with bangs") that she inserted and extended in the completed version of her narrative, which appears in figure 5.4 with the material from this lesson in italicized text. As I discuss at length in chapter 6, the presence of these concrete details about Barbie's appearance opened up space for important reflection during a one-to-one conference I had with Sahra over the draft.

Janice and Billy's interactive modeling set both of these productive composing events in motion. With her sketch Janice showed how to capture an image with just enough detail to prompt conversation. With his questions Billy showed how to convey genuine interest in the story a peer had to tell. Janice's use of the exchange in her subsequent composing demonstrated how writers can take advantage of peer feedback without surrendering ownership of their work. The staff collaboration led to peer collaboration that resulted in improved text for students like Kevin and Sahra.

Multiple models offered by multiple teachers, working individually and in pairs, helped put to rest most, if not all, of the concerns about the approach that first surfaced during the academic-year PD at Robinson. Taking up the stance of "Let me show you how I do this"—or, in the case of the interactive modeling, "how *we* do this"—allowed staff to provide the explicitness that many youth needed to understand and apply new skills and strategies. That we participated alongside students in informal activities and shared our emergent writing, including text we deleted or revised, helped prevent that modeling from positioning us as distant, infallible experts. At its best the institute allowed adults and youth to be members of the same community, all concerned with

FIGURE 5.4   Sahra's completed personal narrative

Americanized Family

"It's here!" I screamed from the front door of our house. It was one of those hot, sunny 90 degree days, but it felt normal because I wasn't in XXX. I was in Nairobi, Kenya. I ran as fast as my little 6 year old legs could take me.

"It's finally here!" I said to my mom. My stepfather sent me a doll back from America. I was happy that he said he would send me anything back. The first thing I asked for was a Barbie doll because it was like the hottest new toy. My friends had some and it was all over the commercials. I wanted the doll because everybody had one and it was everywhere. But I think Barbie sort of represented America at the time and I wanted to feel like I was in America, even before I got here. She was so much different than everyone around me.

The doll arrived on a wedding day, so the house was in chaos. There were clothes and shoes and other things scattered everywhere. My aunt, my mom's cousin, was getting married and she was getting ready at our house. We found out that my dad also sent clothes and other things. My mom gave me the box. I immediately tore the striped wrapper and there she was. *The Barbie doll was BEAUTIFUL! She had curly blond hair with bangs and a light pink dress with high heels and a pink purse.* She also came with a pink brush, a white blouse, a hot pink skirt and black boots.

When I opened the box it felt like time had stopped and everyone was just looking at her and me. After what felt like forever, I took her out and went to go show it to my best friend, but my mother told me to get ready for the wedding and that I could play with her tomorrow. So I ran to my room to get dressed. I was going to wear my white dress with gold threading on it. I was happy because I was going to have my hair curled.

The wedding was going to be in a tent outside our house. We lived on the bottom floor of an apartment building. When I got there only the early birds were there. The tent was beautiful. There were streamers and flowers and flower petals all over the place. The wedding night was great. There was traditional Somali music and Kenyan music with traditional dancing. And some of my best friends were there. I told them all about my new doll, and they all wanted to see it. I told them to come tomorrow. At about 10 o'clock my mother told me to go inside the house and sleep, because I had school the next day.

That next day felt like the longest day ever. I was dazed all day and very anxious to go home. When I got home I was so excited. I didn't even change out of my uniform (a checkered blue and white dress with pants and a white head scarf) and I ran into our small shared bedroom. But the horror that awaited me couldn't compare with anything I could imagine, not even the assassination of Abraham Lincoln.

I opened the box and, AHHHHHHHHHHHH!! My beloved Barbie doll had a broken head. The first thing I did was scream. My mom came in from the kitchen. She asked what was wrong and I told her my Barbie was broken.

FIGURE 5.4 Sahra's completed personal narrative *(continued)*

"Honey, don't be a drama queen about it," was what she said.

I felt like ripping *her* head off. Then my mom told me to ask my younger sister. I didn't want to because I really didn't like her. I went outside to where she was and asked if she knew what happened.

"Hey, do you know what happened to my doll?" I asked.

"Why would I know what happened?" she replied.

And then I saw it, along with her other toys of kitchen plates and such. I remembered that she had also got a doll (but hers wasn't as great as mine). Her doll, at the moment, didn't have a head.

"Hey, how come mine and yours, both, don't have a head? Did you break mine because you broke yours?!"

"Maybe," she said in a small voice.

I didn't say anything else. All I wanted to do was run off and die somewhere (drama queen?) My sister broke my Barbie, my connection to America and to my dad. She ruined my idea of beauty. She took away my chance at feeling like everybody else.

I ran into the disinfectant-smelling bathroom and cried for what felt like hundreds of years (yet, it was only half an hour). When I came back out I saw that my doll was in one piece. No one told me anything, so I didn't say anything.

I later found out that my mom and sister put tape on it. I was daddy's girl and that doll meant so much to me. I knew they felt bad that they had hurt me. My family had learned what mattered to me, and so did I.

learning more about writing. The program's guest writer component, discussed next, offered an experience that supported those goals for both staff and students.

Mentoring

This section addresses the mentoring roles that guest writers from the community played in the institute. I share how we identified these guests and what insights they offered before discussing the approaches we used to amplify the impact of their presentations on youth participants. I use the term *mentoring* here rather than *modeling* to indicate that while a few guest writers, including James Rolling, brought artifacts to support concrete demonstrations, most guests focused on sharing general processes and experiences that inspired new ways of thinking about writing rather than demonstrated particular skills or strategies.

Who We Invited and What They Offered

The institute's guest writer component was born partway through Year 1 after students selected topics for digital stories. As students framed inquiry questions related to those topics, it struck us that many groups would benefit from access to first-person perspectives. To facilitate this, we invited people of our acquaintance with relevant expertise—including several newspaper journalists, a college volleyball player, a playwright, and a stand-up comic—to connect with students. Several arranged to exchange information electronically or by phone, but local sports columnist Bud Poliquin volunteered to speak in person. Because so many participants' first-day surveys expressed interest in sports writing, we made his presentation program-wide and scheduled it during opening meeting.

Notebook entries and our observations indicated that students found Poliquin's talk captivating. They laughed when he recounted trying to please his first boss, a visually impaired newspaper editor who exhorted his employees to write with enough vivid detail to "make me see." They were impressed that writing had taken him to twenty-four Final Four tournaments, sixteen Super Bowls, and seven World Series. And they were intrigued by his argument that writing, unlike sports, "is the fairest thing you can do," because "nobody in the room has more letters—twenty-six [in English]—than the next guy," all writers fail repeatedly, and all writers can get better from hard work. His messages resonated so well with the institute audience, adults and youth alike, that we scheduled two more program-wide presentations by other guest writers that year. (We also invited Bud back for the next three years, making him the only guest writer to present during all four iterations.)

Before the next year's implementation, we systematized guest writers as a program component. We developed a process for assembling four or five guest sessions per year that we used consistently from then on. The process involved brainstorming a list of possible guests during May and June and then assigning staff members with the closest connection to each invitee to make the pitch and schedule a presentation date. Each year we took care to construct a varied slate of guests. (See table 5.1 for an overview.)

Guest presentations typically lasted thirty to forty-five minutes, with an additional fifteen minutes reserved for a question-and-answer period. They took place during opening meeting every two to three days to

TABLE 5.1   Guest writers

Name	Year(s)	Profession	Ethnicity and Gender	Language Background
Bud Poliquin	1, 2, 3, 4	Sportswriter	White male	Monolingual
Donna Ditota	1	Sportswriter	White female	Monolingual
Cedric Bolton	1	Spoken word poet	African American male	Monolingual
James Rolling	2, 3	Artist and picture book author	African American male	Monolingual
Nader Maroun	2	City councilor	Arab American male	Multilingual
Maureen Green	2	Television anchor	White female	Monolingual
Neal Powless	3	Film consultant	Native American male	Multilingual
Elise Ginkel, Katelyn Kanavy, and Crystal Rhode	3	Marketing professionals for engineering firm	White females	Monolingual
Katharine Chang	3, 4	Pediatrician	Asian American female	Multilingual
Tula Goenka	4	Documentary film producer	Southeast Asian American female	Multilingual
Robert Wilson and a student panel	4	Director of supportive services program and a sampling of university students enrolled in it	Varied	Multilingual

permit other kinds of whole-group instruction, including teacher modeling, on the other days. We sought to complete them within the first two weeks so that students could draw on ideas from guests when they chose topics and conducted research for digital stories, activities that mostly took place during the final week.

Guest writers' presentations offered a number of benefits. Because they represented different ethnicities and language backgrounds, their participation helped convey an inclusive message about who identifies as a writer. The diversity of their professions went even further, demonstrating varied purposes for writing in the workplace and in the community. City councilor Nader Maroun talked about writing to communicate with constituents and craft legislation to make change. (He also shared a poignant story about the "treasure" of his Arabic-speaking parents' journals dating from 1900, the year they immigrated to the US.) Student affairs professional Cedric Bolton described using his passion for poetry to engage undergraduates in his work. Pediatrician Katharine Chang explained how physicians document patients' histories and physical examinations with clear writing to ensure coordinated care by all members of a medical team. She also talked about writing letters to officials working in child protective services to advocate for families when needed. With these examples, all three guests framed writing as having real-world purposes and consequences far more varied than what most students cited in their first-day responses to our EQ-focused prompt.

Guest writers also demonstrated that writing takes varied forms, sharing perspectives aligned with the institute's emphases on multimodal, not just print, composing. Year 3, for instance, featured several presentations reinforcing an expanded conception of writing. Artist and art educator James Rolling returned to share new work marrying visual images with narrative text. Former television news anchor Maureen Green discussed her transition into the world of blogging. Neal Powless spoke about his work as a producer, cultural consultant, and technical expert on *Crooked Arrows*, the first Hollywood film to focus on the game of lacrosse through the eyes of the Native Americans who invented it. He screened a video clip and showed students storyboards he used to choreograph the lacrosse action scenes. These guests and others over the years helped reinforce the importance of the sketching we asked students to do in their writer's notebooks and of the multimodal planning tools we offered for their digital stories.

Finally, guest writers mentored participants' understanding of writing as a collaborative endeavor. For instance, three members of a local engineering firm's marketing department assigned students to groups for exercises in designing a tagline and logo for a hypothetical school snack bar. They explained that composing in marketing is typically done by teams collaborating with one another as well as with clients. Tula Goenka, a film producer working in both her native India and the US, talked about filmmaking as collective activism that depends on "teamwork by the hundreds of people" listed "if you've ever sat all the way through the credits at the end." Such ideas reinforced the overall community ethos of our program, and they were applicable to the collaborative work students were doing with digital stories.

How We Amplified Guest Writers' Mentorship

Leveraging the mentoring contributions of guest writers was about more than just selecting the right people and getting out of their way, however. It also depended on deliberate instructional moves our team made and refined with subsequent program iterations. Some moves happened prior to guests' arrival, while others scaffolded students' learning during and after the visits.

We used several approaches to prepare students for productive interactions with our guests. On the day before the first presentation, staff led whole-program discussion of this question: "What does it look like and sound like to be an attentive, interested audience member?" In Years 3 and 4 we asked students to brainstorm scenarios in and out of school when people might ask each other interview questions (e.g., television news programs, family history projects, etc.). We then offered question-framing tips like these that Neva, one of the most prolific note takers from Year 3, captured in this way:

- Avoid [questions] that can be answered with a yes/no answer
- Try not to be too personal
- Follow up [a] general question with a more specific one if you need the answer still
- Be a little more formal in your language if you don't know the person well.

These lessons enhanced the guest writer component while also validating and developing interpersonal skills around interviewing that were valuable for high school and beyond.

To help students translate generic interviewing advice into specific questions for a guest, we shared a photograph and brief biography of each person. Students used this background information to brainstorm potential questions that staff recorded on the LGIR whiteboard. After a group discussion of which questions might best launch the Q&A, we designated two volunteers to ask them, preventing awkward silence. Once the ice was broken, most kids were comfortable enough to contribute without further teacher orchestration, although leaving the list of questions on display allowed students who were shyer or less confident about their English to use it as a reference. On occasion, teachers asked questions themselves, particularly if they knew something important about a guest writer's profile that had not yet emerged.

In Year 2 we also began to scaffold students' note taking during guest presentations with more precision. These lessons were sparked by our discovery during afternoon planning of several detailed entries that took different approaches from each other. (See figure 5.5 for an example from Jilly.) We displayed copies of these entries during opening meeting and invited individuals whose notes were sparse to consider adopting some of the peers' strategies, including bullets, abbreviations, and direct quotations. The strong models had an immediate impact, with numerous participants capturing significantly more detail in their next set of notes as well as experimenting with different ways to organize them. Not surprisingly, display and discussion of note-taking exemplars from peers in previous iterations became a standard feature of our instructional routines before our first guest's visit each year.

In addition to asking students to review these notes to guide completion of entries in the EQ chart discussed in chapters 3 and 4, we built references to ideas from guests' presentations into subsequent days of instruction. More than a full week after Bud Poliquin's visit, for example, we asked students to reflect on whether they felt they were "mentally tired" at the end of the previous day's composing. This prompt re-invoked Bud's assertion that "if you're not tired after you write, you're not working hard enough. There has to be some energy expended." As a follow-up to Nader Maroun's advice that students monitor their interactions for opportunities to support one another, we asked them to give public praise to peers who had helped them solve writing challenges during a given day. (See more on this in chapter 7.) Exchanges like these reinforced the importance of guest writers' presentations, framing them as a significant instructional component and not just an isolated special event.

We further amplified the impact of guest writers' mentoring by designing additional opportunities for reflective writing about the visits. Beginning in Year 2 we posted graffiti charts in the LGIR for each guest and encouraged both teachers and students to mine their notes for memorable quotations to share. When possible, we displayed a sample text by the guest—a letter to the editor by Maroun, a blog post by Green—next

FIGURE 5.5 Note-taking exemplar from Jilly

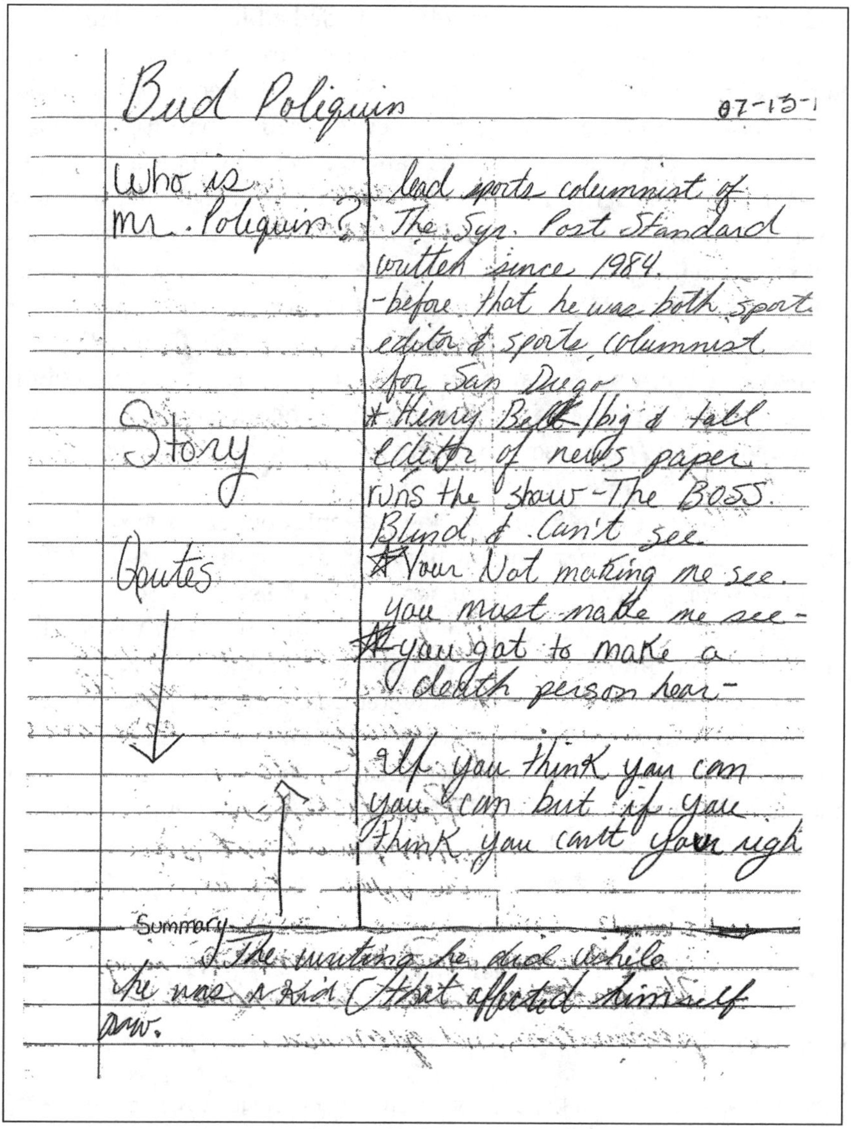

Bud Poliquin 07-13-1

Who is Mr. Poliquin? | lead sports columnist of The Syr. Post Standard written since 1984.
-before that he was both sport editor & sports columnist for San Diego

Story | *Henry Belk/big & tall editor of news paper runs the show - The BOSS. Blind & Can't see

Qoutes | *Your Not making me see. you must make me see - *you got to make a death person hear-
If you think you can you can but if you think you can't your righ

Summary
The writing he did while he was a kid that affected himself now.

to the chart to further illustrate variations in each guest's purpose and audience for writing.

The graffiti charts also served as an important prewriting tool when we realized, also in Year 2, that we had been missing an authentic opportunity for students to write in another real-world genre: the formal letter of thanks. We began to recruit small groups of student volunteers to draft such letters to send to our guests, which yielded additional practice with collaborative authorship that we saw as parallel to what group construction of digital stories required. Those who volunteered to work on the letters took their notebooks and the relevant graffiti chart to the Robinson cafeteria, where many students gathered before the program's official start at 9 a.m. Each letter typically required one or two early morning sessions to compose on a designated teacher's laptop, with that adult embedded in the group to guide the process with the lightest touch possible. Although the finished letters were often not long (see figure 5.6 for an example), they reflected considerable investment by their authors.

Also worth noting is that, over time, the composition of the volunteer groups changed in ways reflecting our increased support for youth from traditionally under-served groups. At first, letter writing was dominated by US-born students with strong technical skills. As we reinforced the importance of note taking during presentations more strongly and encouraged a wider swath of our population to contribute to the Q&A, the groups reflected more heterogeneous skill levels and varied language backgrounds. The crowning example of this pattern was in Year 4 when Jadwa, a Somali immigrant who uttered fewer than a half dozen English words during our first week, volunteered to be among those writing a thank-you to Tula Goenka, the Indian-born filmmaker. This move represented important risk taking for Jadwa, and it was not lost on us that she chose to join a group for which other English learners had already volunteered nor that the letter's recipient was, like herself, multilingual.

FIGURE 5.6   Letter of thanks to guest writer

Dear Mr. Powless,

We would like to thank you for taking time out of your job to come and talk about why you write. In your presentation we liked the fact that you mentioned how much pride you have in your race and culture. And we especially liked how you corrected people respectfully about stereotypes.

Sincerely,

Robinson Early College High School Students

Adult mentoring and modeling played important roles in supporting youth participants in the institute to construct stronger writing identities—to develop a sense of their agency as writers and to sharpen their use of skills and strategies to enact that agency. Students valued this program feature, as indicated by a comment from an exit survey by Janie in Year 4: "I liked when we had guest speakers come in and tell us about writing. . . . I also liked listening to adults' insights on how writing is important in the world."

Students were not the only ones who benefited from modeling and mentoring in shared space, however. Doing this work collaboratively in shared space increased the adults' capacity as well. Staff gleaned new insights about scaffolding writing for a heterogeneous group of learners from co-planning and co-teaching lessons with one another, as well as from observing other people's modeling in the LGIR. All of us learned more about writing's potential impact in the world from interacting with guest writers pursuing varied professions and passions beyond the school walls.

Tips and Takeaways

Although Jake was once a vociferous critic of modeling, his multiple stints on the institute staff led to a change of heart and a change in the academic-year practice he reported. During an interview, he shared, with a bit of amusement, his satisfaction that one of his freshmen had commented that very day: "Oh, wait a minute. I get what you're doing. You're showing us exactly the way you want us to do things." As you work to model and mentor writing in your own context, consider the following:

- *Complete assigned writing tasks yourself.* Save artifacts of your process, not just the finished products, to integrate into your modeling.
- *Keep think-alouds about your writing process short and focused.* In the institute, the most effective modeling lasted no more than five to ten minutes without an opportunity for students to share their impressions or try a new skill on their own in their notebooks. Make sure students can see your text from their seats and that they are not just listening to you talk about it.

- *Survey students about their professional interests.* Some of our best ideas for guest writers were initiated by students' responses to a question we asked about what they envisioned they'd be doing in ten years.
- *Brainstorm guest possibilities with other colleagues, even if you are teaching alone.* A collaborative process for identifying invitees will create a more diverse list than you can generate alone. Possible categories to consider include:
  - alumni of your school, including current university students who can discuss the writing demands of majors that secondary schools do not typically offer
  - local business owners
  - family members of enrolled students or staff
  - fellow teachers with side or summer businesses or who pursued other careers before entering teaching

CHAPTER 6

Conferring with Student Writers

I t's Monday, Day 6 of Year 4, and afternoon planning is about to begin. Most students made considerable headway today with their personal narratives, and teachers conducted one-to-one conferences with nearly all of them. The warm-up prompt on the whiteboard is intended to spark discussion of those interactions: "Write about a conference you had today that moved a kid forward. Who was it with, and what made it work?"

After seven or eight minutes of silent writing, staff share highlights from their entries. Sue describes an interaction with Marwa, a native Arabic speaker diagnosed with a traumatic brain injury. In Sue's view Marwa was trying to "tell two different stories in the same piece," one about an accident her father had and the other about her family's move to America from Iraq. Sue says it was helpful to ask Marwa to organize her ideas more tightly in her writer's notebook before returning to the keyboard to draft more text. Rebecca also reports using the notebook to help a student get unstuck, but in a different way. Denisha, a US-born Black girl identified with a learning disability in written language, was struggling to apply an opening-meeting lesson on leads to a story about losing both grandfathers in the same year—experiences still emotionally raw for her. Observing that Denisha was "close to tears," Rebecca reports choosing to write down lead possibilities in the girl's notebook for her as they talked. She thinks the entry will help Denisha with a "fresh start tomorrow," after she has had a chance to compose herself.

During the sharing, I keep notes on the whiteboard about instructional moves each person describes that others might adopt or adapt during subsequent conferences. Later I insert these notes into the next day's collective plan to remind staff about options they might use with students:

- Have them go back to their notebooks to list more details, draft more text, or organize the text they have in a new way.
- Use the highlighting tool in Microsoft Word to help them organize text into paragraphs.
- Show them how to identify action sentences in their text and to put sticky notes nearby to add information about their thoughts and feelings associated with the actions.
- Embed questions in kids' text.
- Use the return key to insert spaces where they need to add details/put in some paragraphs.

Although the notes are brief, they communicate clearly to those of us who took part in the discussion. Each option will be used by more than one staff member over the remaining two weeks of the program.

I open with this vignette because it illustrates the importance of conferences in addressing the varying needs of the institute's heterogeneous population. In the pages that follow, I explain why conferences—intentional, personalized exchanges in service of learning between a teacher and a student writer or, in the case of the digital stories, a student group composing together—were central to the institute's design. I discuss how our staff's understandings and enactments of conferences evolved over multiple iterations. I focus, in particular, on how collaboration in various forms influenced staff use of an instructional approach that has often been framed as a solo endeavor.

Why We Embraced Conferring

Teacher-led writing conferences with individual students have been a staple of resources on process-focused writing instruction for more than three decades now. Proponents argue that conferences strengthen relationships between adults and youth, illuminate student intentions for their texts, provide personalized feedback to support new learning, and yield data to inform instruction in small-group and whole-class formats.[1] Although conferences, like writer's notebooks, have rarely been the dedicated focus of peer-reviewed research on writing instruction, practitioners connected to a number of research-based networks have provided detailed, nuanced descriptions of conferences and documented their impact on individual students' writing development. Some of the best-known accounts of conferring take place in contexts with limited linguistic and cultural diversity, however, and most include little information about classroom roles played by paraprofessionals and special education teachers.

I was aware of these trends in the professional literature when I constructed the document that guided academic-year PD at Robinson and, eventually, the writing institute design. "Conducting planful (not just spontaneous) writing conferences" was an element in this action plan because of my suspicion, based on my own research and reports from preservice teacher candidates, that many teachers in the region used conferences more often as a management tool—to clarify a task and monitor behavior—than as an instructional tool to develop writing skills and strategies. Consequently, I organized one of our PD sessions on such topics as creating a yearlong conference plan to promote greater independence for students over time and selecting a conference format based on instructional purposes. (See table 6.1 for one of the handouts we discussed.)

The discussions during that session revealed that Robinson teachers saw conferences as valuable and that nearly all sought to conduct them regularly. Several participants described enlisting help from student teachers or push-in special education staff when possible to make it easier to meet with individual writers. Yet the conversation also revealed that conferences were a source of frustration for many. Teachers worried about addressing challenging group behavior when they were occupied with one student and no other adults were present. They reported struggling to extricate themselves from lengthy conferences with needy writers, particularly with learners new to English. Those who commented on student drafts at length before conferences found such preparation time-consuming and hard to sustain. As Rebecca explained later, when sharing a conference-related professional goal during Year 4, conferring was always something she wanted to do more regularly, but it was "always the first thing to go when things get busy."

The launch of the writing institute allowed the Year 1 staff and me to tackle these conference-related concerns directly and collaboratively. We sought that summer, and over the next three iterations, to develop conferring principles and practices that drew on existing conference literature while accounting more explicitly for (1) the needs of a

TABLE 6.1   Conference comparison handout from Robinson PD

Teacher-Directed Writing Conferences

Conference Type	Advance Preparation	Benefits	Constraints/Problems to Solve
On the Fly (less than a minute per student)	• Minimal	• Allows for large number of students to be seen • Heads off problems and misconceptions in advance	• Can't be very thorough or deep • Can be difficult to extricate oneself from needy students • Requires quick reading of student texts and fast decision-making
Planned One-to-One (two to five minutes)	• Typically requires teachers to review student work in advance, although it can also be student-initiated	• Helps to build relationships between teacher and students • Very targeted to individual students' needs • Easier to assess student understanding on the spot	• Time consuming to schedule • Can be awkward, especially with shy students • Can be difficult to extricate oneself from needy students • More chance of teacher doing too much of the talking
Small-Group (five to fifteen minutes)	• Works best when teachers specify student groupings in advance • Requires designated instructional focus, often determined from reading student work from an entire class	• More efficient to schedule • Allows for peer interaction and engagement around skill or strategy being taught • Offers a site for follow-up related to skill or strategy when teacher moves on	• Less individualized attention • Can be difficult to pitch the instruction at the right level for all members • Group talk can sometimes mask lack of understanding by one member

multilingual population whose skills and experiences varied widely and (2) a secondary school context where curriculum was organized around required units rather than an ongoing reading-writing workshop. That the institute kept some school-year constraints in play (e.g., some students with major skill gaps, aging technology) while reducing others (e.g., student-teacher ratio, grading expectations) created a space to test conference solutions that we hoped would yield new insights for all of us, perhaps even leading to academic-year traction.

Common Tools to Support Conferring

Although staff had brief exchanges over students' notebook entries during opening or closing meetings in the LGIR, the vast majority of conferences took place during instruction led by teaching teams in the classrooms and computer labs. Most instructional sessions featured at least an hour of composing related to one of the focal genres, and our collective plans typically called for staff to conduct either planned or on-the-fly conferences during this period. It was common for us to divide that composing period into two chunks, with a five-to-ten-minute break in the middle for what Cris Tovani calls "the catch," a focused tip or demonstration based on "patterns of understanding or confusion the teacher notices as she confers with individuals and groups."[2] During many days, particularly near the end of the program when we were keenly concerned with students completing products to share at the celebration, additional staff such as Mary Taylor, Bryan Crandall, and I joined the teams to increase the number of adults available to confer.

From Year 1 on, we used two common tools to support conferences: (1) a strengths-first structured protocol and (2) a conference record-keeping form. Although we refined our use of these tools over time, their essential features remained consistent across all four iterations.

Using a Strengths-First Structured Protocol

Our strengths-first structured protocol was informed by Lucy Calkins's well-known recommendation to "teach the writer, not the writing."[3] It was intended to encourage student growth and independence and to discourage adults from applying a "fix-it" mentality to student texts that could easily slide into deficit-oriented thinking, particularly for the least skilled or experienced writers on our roster. The protocol thus required staff to identify and name one strength about the piece of writing at the center of the conference, usually shared first, and one suggestion for improvement, often described as the "next step." The conference could include other elements, as described at the beginning of this chapter, but it had to include those two, regardless of whether it was planned or on the fly. If the conference was planned, the teacher would make notes for herself in advance about what she wanted to share in each category. If it was on the fly, the interaction might be sequenced differently, particularly if initiated by a student, but the expectation was the same. Before moving on to interact with another student, the teacher would point out something she liked about the text and make (or validate) a suggestion for improvement.

We were scrupulous about naming strengths for several reasons that benefited learners. Students who were metacognitively aware of what they were doing well as writers—and who had language to talk about those strengths with others—were better equipped to maintain and even refine those skills than students who lacked such awareness. Specific and sincere praise was also motivating for learners, as the literature on feedback predicts.[4] In the institute such praise appeared to be particularly beneficial for students with a history of struggle in school for one reason or another. Kristina, the Year 2 staff member who knew many participants from having taught them in middle school, shared her pleasant surprise about dramatic improvements she saw in numerous individuals' behavior and engagement during the institute: "I was flabbergasted . . . that these were the same kids." She attributed those shifts to the impact of consistent praise about specific features of students' writing as opposed to the "constant critiquing" many faced in school.

Our use of "next step" language, including how we encoded it for our own reference, was similarly positive. When we recorded a suggestion on a sticky note—regardless of whether the note was for adult reference or for sharing with a student—we used an arrow symbol to indicate that the item was for consideration in the future. We avoided describing either the writing or the writer as having weaknesses and eschewed use of the minus symbol, which might have seemed a natural inverse to the plus sign with which we often tagged strengths. These choices were about more than semantics; they were intentional framings of writing improvement as within reach for all learners, although the timetables for development might differ.

The requirement to generate just one strength and one next step for every participant was also crucial. Maintaining that balance supported teacher capacity building in terms of differentiation and further diverted deficit perspectives. With skilled, experienced writers, it was easy to identify strengths but often harder to identify next steps that would be appropriately challenging. With less fluent writers, particularly those new to English, it was tempting to cut immediately to all the issues needing attention, skipping right past the identification of aspects to celebrate, including those too small or subtle to register on a standardized assessment. The parallel structure of the protocol kept us honest, helping to ensure that we commended accomplishment while planning for continuous improvement. This was important for all kids, but it was essential for those from demographic groups whose potential as writers has been historically overlooked, even denied, in school.[5]

The stripped-down nature of the strengths-first protocol was also linked to our desire to design tools and processes that would be sustainable for teachers amid the competing concerns of the school year. This meant envisioning expectations for interactions that were regular and student-centered but perhaps less leisurely and open-ended than the conferences described in much of the professional literature. Institute staff and I could see the value of extended exchanges organized around Carl Anderson's iconic "How's it going?" invitation, and we typically sought students' perspectives on their work before we shared our own thoughts on strengths and next steps.[6] But we conjectured that teachers subject to the larger class sizes and crowded curriculum mandates of secondary school would be more likely to maintain use of a quick, clearly focused tool than they would be to enact broad principles improvisationally, especially if they had limited ongoing support for the latter.

The protocol also meant changes in how teachers conceptualized their preparation for those interactions. Some staff members, particularly in Year 1, confessed to feeling negligent if they did not offer copious marginal feedback and comprehensive error correction on students' drafts. Their conscientiousness as professionals and their awareness of the stakes attached to state scrutiny of poor student outcomes made it hard to do otherwise. To support them in reconsidering this practice, which a famously comprehensive meta-analysis by George Hillocks presents as burdensome to teachers with little learner benefit,[7] I reviewed printed drafts for thirty personal narratives, ten from each dyad, at the close of Week 2. I chose papers in various stages of completion, taking care to include students from each dyad who varied in terms of skill and experience. After reading the drafts quickly, without a pen in my hand to curb my own editing impulses, I recorded a strength and a next step on a sticky note for each kid. (See figure 6.1 for a sampling.) During afternoon planning, I invited the dyad teams to read the same drafts after me, using the protocol to generate their own ideas about what feedback would be helpful before comparing their notes with mine to determine a conference plan for the following day. Although the process yielded a good deal of consensus about how to proceed with individual learners, its most significant outcome was the license it gave several staff members to take up a new stance toward student drafts. As Sue explained, "What helped me was when Kelly said *focus on one thing*. I could give one comment that could focus the student. If you see an improvement, keep going. I don't [have to] spend so much time fixing everything."

In Year 2 we retained the multi-reader focus approach to conference preparation but minimized my role as program director, eliciting multiple perspectives on each piece of work from across the staff. At least two different adults read each student's draft using the strengths-first protocol. Dyad partners worked together to determine which pieces of feedback would be shared—and by whom—during conferences the next day. An extended example from one student, Dayton, reveals the generativity of this approach. Dayton was a US-born Black boy whose personal narrative was about the impact of getting glasses, then contacts, on his life in and out of school. Jake, to whose dyad Dayton was assigned, read and wrote the first sticky note about the draft:

> You paint a nice picture of what it's like to get glasses (I always wanted them growing up), and you capture the emotion of the experience very nicely. Focus on fixing some grammar/punctuation issues and the flow of the story.
>
> *Mr. P.*

Mary served as the second reader for Dayton's draft, providing this feedback:

> Getting contacts really changed your life. You have lots of sensory language—"blurry," "dusty."
> Can you tell your story with a focus on your eyesight?
>
> *Mrs. Taylor*

FIGURE 6.1 Samples of sticky-note planning for conferences

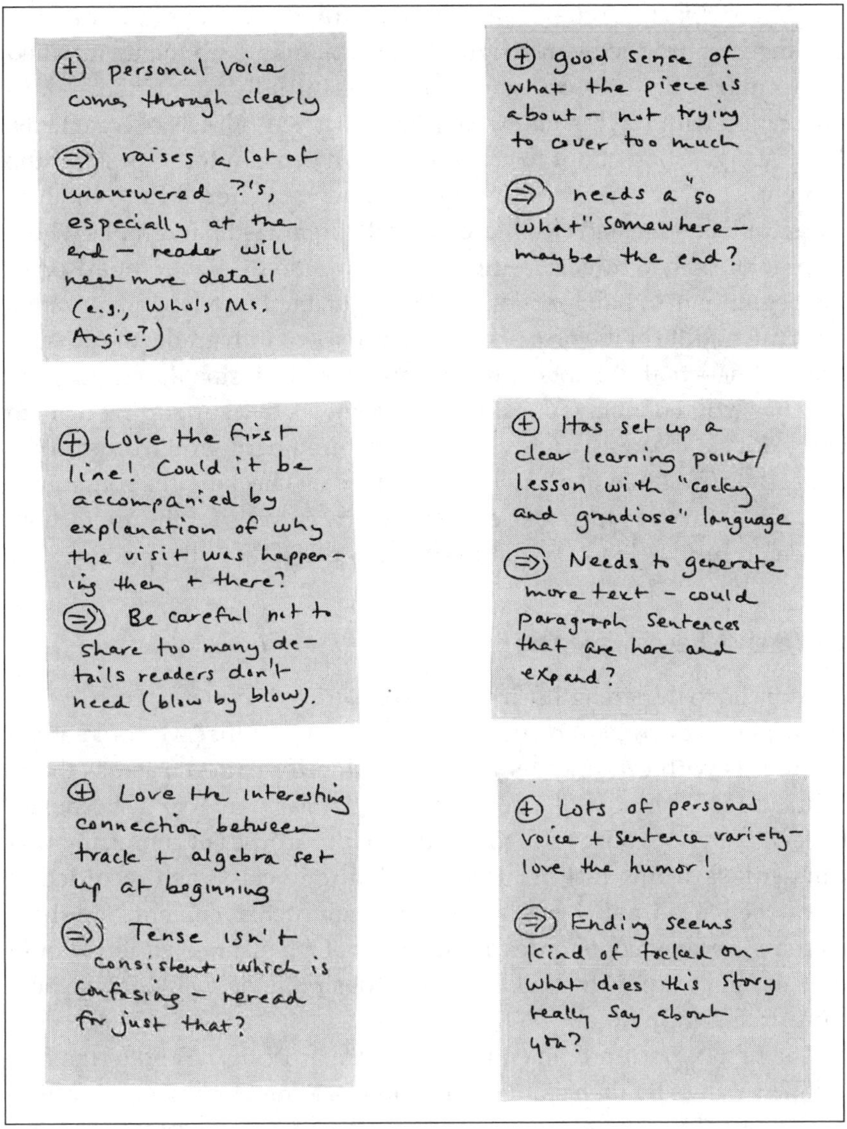

The opportunity to compare (literal) notes with Mary helped Jake shape and enact a conference plan that supported Dayton in making a number of productive revisions. Instead of taking up the unspecified "grammar/punctuation issues" that he initially identified, Jake's interaction with Dayton followed a thread across both sets of comments: Mary's suggestion about focus and his own concern for flow. After the conference, Dayton cut vague and extraneous material from the first paragraph and created two more logically organized paragraphs where he previously had three. (See figure 6.2 for a side-by-side comparison of the beginnings of both versions.) He also deleted two long paragraphs from the middle of the piece—one a summary of fifth grade, the other of sixth grade—that did not explicitly pertain to the vision theme. Anyone who has worked with young adolescents knows that supporting them to cut text is no mean feat. Once they've captured hard-won words on the page, they are often loath to lose them! Cross-checking his conference plan with Mary's helped Jake establish a clearer focus for the interaction, which, in turn, helped Dayton to streamline and focus the piece.

Conference Record-Keeping Forms

In addition to the strengths-first protocol, we used common record-keeping forms to document conference interactions so that we could share highlights with one another as well as identify patterns across them. I introduced the idea of a conference form early in Year 1, because I believed its use would foreground the dual purposes of conferring that can get lost during task-focused circulating in class. As I recorded in my reflective journal, it was important to conduct, document, and share learning, because conferences, particularly of the planned variety, would help us "get to know the kids' needs" and, simultaneously, "move them forward" as individuals.

The first opportunity to employ the form arose at the end of the first week in Year 1. By then students had brainstormed topics for their digital stories. Many expressed excitement about pursuing personal interests rather than being limited to predetermined areas of the curriculum. We worried, however, that some of their interests were too broad, lacking a clear connection to the writing-focused EQs. During afternoon planning, Janice proposed that our goal the next day should be helping kids develop a "narrower sense of their digital story." To that end, we designed opening meeting with three parts: (1) pairs of teachers

FIGURE 6.2 Comparing Dayton's beginnings

Pre-Conference Version	Post-Conference Version
It was the fourth grade year and everyone was back in school. ~~I saw all my friends again and everyone was happy. This year was different because in past years people would be a lot happier. I had no idea what was going on.~~ School was very important too me. I couldn't focus so much in class so I did better in resource. My fourth grade teacher was very hard on us about everything we did. I needed too get my grades up drastically. In the middle of the year my friend got kicked out of school. This gave me a better opportunity to focus a little more in class. I was ready too committing to school. I was the kid that always sat in the back. My desk was far away from the chalkboard. I never really thought anything of it as it wasn't a big deal, but as I started to pay attention more, I noticed my eyesight was terrible. Every day that went by was like I'd been staring at the sun for years. The board was so blurry, dusty, and just not clearly visible. I couldn't see, but I tried keeping a good mood. I asked my teacher if I could move up multiple times, but it was like everything I was saying went through one ear and out the other. Even through this, I tried to remain happy, but soon the happiness turned into frustration.	It was the fourth grade year and everyone was back in school. School was very important to me, but I couldn't focus so much in class. I did better in resource. My fourth grade teacher was very hard on us about everything we did. I needed to get my grades up drastically. In the middle of the year my friend got kicked out of school. This gave me a better opportunity to focus a little more in regular class. I was ready to commit to school. I was the kid that always sat in the back. My desk was far away from the chalkboard. I never really thought anything of it as it wasn't a big deal, but as I started to pay attention more, I noticed my eyesight was terrible. Every day that went by was like I'd been staring at the sun for years. The board was so blurry, dusty, and just not clearly visible. I couldn't see, but I tried keeping a good mood. I asked my teacher if I could move up multiple times, but it was like everything I was saying went through one ear and out the other. Even through this, I tried to remain happy, but soon the happiness turned into frustration.

modeling how to identify connections between proposed digital story topics and writing, (2) students recording ideas about their topics in their writer's notebooks, and (3) pairs of students sharing and refining their ideas with each other, using the format modeled by the teachers.

I suggested that one way to evaluate the impact of this meeting and determine next steps was to keep conference notes as we interacted with students later in the day. The team agreed, and we added the following note to the collective plan: "Teachers, including Bryan, Kelly and Mary, conduct 1–1 conferences as unobtrusively as possible with students about their topics for digital stories, helping them to shape them." I made copies of a simple four-column form for team members to pick up along with the daily plan, and staff brought completed forms to afternoon planning. (See figure 6.3 for an example from Mary.)

When we discussed the information we gathered via the sheets, several patterns emerged. A high percentage of 2 and 3 strength-of-topic ratings across our sheets suggested that the opening meeting lesson had been generally quite effective in helping students narrow their topics and link them to the EQs, although the students with 1 ratings would likely need some close monitoring. And many students were curious about intersections between writing and media/technology, which offered flexibility to make groups addressing interest while promoting new social relationships (more on this in chapter 7). We drew on both patterns to finalize group assignments and to plan students' first interactions with each other once those groups were unveiled.

Over the years we used variations of the form to support conferring for assorted purposes. On some days no explicit focus was stipulated; staff simply recorded whatever struck them as important during their interactions with students. On other days we used the forms to document information in predetermined categories. We rated students' success in addressing the "So what" question with their personal narrative drafts (which helped us identify some strong peer examples to share in opening meeting). We tracked the completeness of digital story scripts (which allowed us to set a schedule for groups ready to audiotape their narration). In Year 3 we wondered which of our idea-generation activities had yielded topics kids actually pursued in their personal narratives, but we struggled to devise a mechanism to answer that question that did not require time-consuming comparison of writer's notebooks with students' drafts. Crystal proposed during afternoon meeting that we "just ask the kids" as part of our regular conferring—a suggestion that met with

FIGURE 6.3 Mary's record-keeping tool

Staff Member _Mary_   7/16

Digital Story Topic Conferences

Student Name(s)	Topic	Topic is: 1=weak, 2=ok, 3=strong	Notes
Charlie	Social networking	2	When was 1st Facebook page? How did pages develop? language?
Shelley	Teens Lead social life thru texting	3	Interview people w/cell phone – could you go a day w/o it?
André	Sports? Basketball?	?	Wants to work with Marvin
Michaela	What sites are available for young people to post writing?	2	Interested in doing an interview

resounding approbation and led to the collective plan excerpted in figure 6.4. In these cases, the forms helped staff gather data about individual learners that could inform full-team afternoon planning.

The forms also supported coordination of adult efforts within the dyads. In Year 1, for instance, Sue and Rebecca regularly compared their sheets in the mornings before the program officially began to discuss what they had learned from each student they saw. After my observations of Jake and Janice's co-teaching revealed that they had strong but differing preferences about planned versus on-the-fly conferences, they used their forms to divvy up their dyad group and set a schedule so that each would confer with half the students in one format on one day before swapping roles the following day. This plan ensured not only that each student was seen regularly by both partners but also that each of them gained valuable practice using the less familiar format. The Year 4 dyad of Janice and Sue decided to sit next to each other during afternoon planning so that they could examine forms and student work conveniently at the same time while mapping out their conference agenda. Another Year 4 pair, Rebecca and Joanna, observed this move by their peers and quickly followed suit. In all of these examples, staff incorporated the record-keeping forms into processes that worked for them, with different teaching teams approaching them differently. The flexibility and the fact that the forms were mediated by talk among staff, not submitted to a central authority to comply with a data-gathering mandate, prevented their use from being seen as a chore or a burden.

Adjustments to Leverage Collaboration

Over time we adjusted some of our conferring tools and routines to take better advantage of the collaboration offered within the institute, much as we had done with our approaches to modeling. Two adjustments were most salient: (1) a collective approach to planning for instruction to be carried out individually, and (2) the practice of embedding notes within students' drafts to document conferences for student and staff reference.

Collective Planning for Individual Enactment

In the early years of the institute, conferences tended to be addressed during afternoon planning by discussing data that staff members captured in their conference record-keeping forms, as described in the opening of

FIGURE 6.4 Planning for conference record keeping

Time	Activity	Location/Personnel	Materials
10:50–11:35	• Decide as a triad whether you want to pull individuals or a small group to do some more formal planning/sequencing of information before they continue to type in narratives • Cue students before they start writing to insert paragraphs where they're needed • Every kid gets a teacher conference with someone • Note on conference form what planning tool yielded each kid's personal narrative topic: 3 words to describe yourself, notebook cover entry, 10 best things/10 worst things activity, deciding what to say • Have them print drafts at the end of the work period so we can review them during planning	Lower lab: Jake, Maddie, & Paul Career center lab: Crystal, Billy, & Lorraine	Copies of conference form for each staff member

this chapter, and by constructing collective plans specifying when such conferences should take place and what their focus, if any, should be. If a pattern emerged, for instance, across our conferences that many students were struggling to integrate material from their internet research into their digital story scripts, we planned instruction to address this need—a noticings session with a strong exemplar, a teacher think-aloud with her own draft—and then tracked the impact of this intervention via a new round of conferring. By Year 3, however, the stability of our tools and routines combined with staff members' greater comfort level with collaboration allowed us to make the conference-related sections of our collective plans more precise and differentiated. We were better able to leverage the full staff's best thinking to address instructional problems raised by one dyad or one teacher about individuals and groups.

Some of the problems we tackled were associated with conferring in shared space itself. As we examined our practices, we realized that our favorable teacher-student ratio and the presence of multiple adults could have unintended negative consequences on student independence. In Year 4, for example, Jake and Maddie raised concerns during afternoon planning about Kiara, a US-born Black girl assigned to their dyad. Judging from her notebook, Kiara was a fairly fluent writer, but her progress was slow with her narrative, an account of getting grounded by her parents after a disastrous report card. Jake, Maddie, and I all recounted similar—and quite lengthy—conferences with Kiara, each yielding just a few new words in her draft, and Billy corroborated Kiara's need for what he called "handholding" from his experience as her track coach. This information sharing led us to conjecture that our lack of coordination was reinforcing, not interrupting, Kiara's desire for adult validation. We decided that she should work with one teacher, not several, on a given day and that the assigned adult should briefly discuss next steps for her piece and then "walk away and return" rather than remain in her presence for further diversionary discussion. Although Kiara's profile did not transform overnight, she increased the duration of her independent composing periods enough to complete her narrative, and her exit survey comments suggested some self-awareness of her greater persistence: "[The institute] made me realize you can't do one final copy then your done you gotta keep editing it." For staff, the collective discussion of her case offered strategies we could employ to avoid over-conferring with students who shared her needs.

With some lessons a collective approach to conference planning helped us make sure that the decisions about which students to see first—and which to leave alone to support independent problem solving—would be determined by the team's interpretation of varied data, not by students' aggressiveness in attracting adult attention. On Day 11 of Year 3, for example, our afternoon discussion about digital story groups' progress turning their online research into scripts led us to specify, by name, which groups needed to be seen early in the next day's composing period. Of particular concern were Malik and Camilla, who shared an interest in their journalism topic but whose strong personalities were affecting their development of consensus around their script content. Staff discussion suggested that Crystal, whose demeanor was direct but nonconfrontational, would be best equipped to support the navigation of the pair's differences. The plan indicated she should confer first with them, while her teammates, Jake and Lorraine, took on two other groups of concern to their triad. Because conferences are not and should not be scripted, the team could not predict with accuracy which of the three adults would be ready first to initiate another conference. The plan was clear, though, that the triad's next instructional priority was a group conducting inquiry into R&B artist Alicia Keys's songwriting processes. A very short note in the lesson plan ("First one done: Neva et al.") served as shorthand to capture the full staff's belief that this group needed a teacher check-in less acutely than the three groups in the "Confer first" list and more acutely than the other groups on the team's roster.

Around this same time, we also began to embed more specific notes in the collective plans about group-recommended approaches to take during conferences, not just who should be seen in what order. Such notes were telegraphic but concrete, as this plan excerpt shows:

Maddie: Hla/Zoya need to highlight newspaper article, might need more guidance with search terms

Hla and Zoya were English learners—one originally from Myanmar, the other from Somalia—constructing a digital story about *Crooked Arrows*, the lacrosse film coproduced by guest writer Neal Powless. The girls' draft script was limited at that point to a restatement of notes they took during Powless's visit, and they were struggling to identify other sources to consult. Full-staff discussion led to a suggestion that they read a preselected article about the making of the film from the local newspaper, which we felt would provide background information to inform a more open-ended internet search for additional resources. Even then, however, the team predicted that Hla and Zoya might need teacher support to select appropriate search terms. Maddie's name in the collective plan meant that she would confer with the girls over the newspaper article reading as well as follow up on their subsequent searching.

What's notable about this example is that the full team of nine members, not just Maddie, was responsible for devising the plan of action. The suggestions were based on data collected over the course of the program by various teachers who had observed or interacted with the two girls. Maddie was tasked with executing the team's vision, but she was not solely accountable for whether the proposed strategies succeeded or failed. The conference plan was the team's, which contributed significantly to the idea, discussed more extensively in chapter 2, that all staff were responsible for all the students in the program, not just the subset with whom they worked most closely at a given time.

Embedded Notes

Another adjustment to leverage collaboration was a practice we came to call embedded notes. As discussed previously, our preparation protocol discouraged teachers from providing extensive written commentary on student drafts, particularly if those comments were intended to guide revision and editing in the teacher's absence. Most of Robinson's rising freshmen struggled to understand and use written feedback unless it was mediated by in-person discussion. Even after some modeling about how to use such feedback, it was not uncommon for students to ignore written commentary from teachers or to address the suggestions in ways that made the draft less effective rather than more so. (These patterns were understandably quite demoralizing for teachers who spent considerable time constructing those comments!) For this reason, we found it more efficient to invest our preparation time with student drafts in selecting a single teaching point that would have the most impact when elaborated and explained in a conference.

As we refined our conferring approaches over several iterations, however, we began to see benefits in leaving a clearer trace in students' drafts of the instruction that took place during those interactions. Although I had initially shied away from embedding notes in student texts because of my fear that it would undercut their independence and authority over their own composing, I came to realize that the opposite was often true, particularly for students with language-related disabilities or those newer to English who struggled to process oral interactions quickly. Students who had clear notes as a reference to guide further idea generation or revision were often able to proceed with less adult assistance, while students who lacked those notes were often the ones seeking more intensive teacher support.

This shift in thinking led to our use of embedded notes—that is, questions and comments a teacher inserted into a digital text while conducting a face-to-face conference with a student or group of students. The staff member captured key aspects of the exchange with learners within a digital version of the narrative or the group script, generally using capitalized text to distinguish her notes from text produced by the author(s). When the teacher moved away, students used the capitalized material as a revision guide, deleting the comments when they had been addressed in one way or another. We did not use this practice with every conference, but it was usually effective when we did employ it.

A quintessential example of embedded notes was a conference I had in Year 4 with Sahra, the student whose personal narrative about receiving a Barbie doll from her stepfather is included in chapter 5. I met with Sahra when she had established a strong personal voice and a logical sequence in her narrative but her "So what" remained murky. She and I sat at her computer together, with the draft on screen in front of us. After complimenting her on several parts I found funny and memorable, I highlighted a sentence—"There was music, food, and dancing"—and asked if Sahra could use less generic examples to ground it better in the Kenyan setting. Sahra pointed to the word "food" on the screen and asked, "Like *sambusas*?" referring to a popular filled pastry in Africa and the Middle East. I confirmed that this was indeed what I meant, encouraged her to make similar substitutions for the other general terms, and typed, "CAN YOU MAKE THIS MORE KENYAN?" right after the sentence as a shorthand reminder. (Later she would add more specific details about the music and the dancing, though she exercised her writerly discretion and opted not to mention the sambusas.)

This initial discussion of culturally specific details led naturally into my broader focus for the conference, sharpening the overall message that Sahra wanted to convey to the reader. To this end I told Sahra that it was interesting to me that her story took place during a wedding when everyone in the family, including her, would have been dressed in their best and most beautiful clothes but that the clothes probably didn't look much like her detailed description of Barbie's. I then pointed to Sahra's last paragraph, which focused on being more patient with the little sister who broke her doll; asked why she thought Barbie was so important to her at the time; and explained that the two ideas weren't clearly connected for me yet as her reader. I embedded "WHY WAS BARBIE SO IMPORTANT TO YOU?" in that final paragraph. After thinking for a moment, Sahra told me that everyone wanted Barbies at the time, when all their dads were in America, and that she saw Barbie as representing her transition from Kenya to America. This was part of why she was so upset with her sister. I asked if she could use the question in caps to help her revise to make that insight clearer in her draft, and she nodded, beginning to type as I moved away. Her next draft included material that spoke directly to her oral sharing, some of it in place of the embedded question, which she deleted, and some of it in a different location of the text, unprompted by the notes. She also chose, again unprompted by an adult, one of those additions as her audiotaped contribution for the all-program digital story we screened at the celebration: "But I think Barbie sort of represented America at the time and I wanted to feel like I was in America, even before I got here. She was so much different than everyone around me." This decision corroborated data from subsequent conferences with Janice and Billy, her dyad teachers, about her satisfaction with the additions she had made to the text.

In this case, and in others, embedded notes helped participants make more complex moves as writers than they likely could have done on their own, supported by face-to-face interaction with adults but not requiring it at all times to make progress. The approach helped us edge students closer to being able to make good independent use of the kind of marginal feedback they would receive regularly from teachers later in their educational careers.

Embedded notes also helped to leverage our commitment in the institute to co-teaching. Not only did the notes cue students about how to proceed, but they also documented the discussion for the adults involved in the next text-based exchange. Sometimes this allowed the next person to reinforce a teaching point that had already been introduced. (We often found that students who resisted suggestions from a single teacher were more willing to address them when two adults were in agreement about the same text feature.) On other occasions the next staff person in line to confer with students could avoid unnecessary duplication of efforts.

An example of the latter comes from Year 4 when Janice was preparing to confer with Bethany, a native English-speaking White girl writing a narrative about her anxious experiences taking and receiving scores from two state-level examinations. When Janice reviewed printed drafts from the students in her dyad, she encountered my embedded notes, as I had been the last person to confer with Bethany. A paragraph in the middle of Bethany's narrative moved very quickly through a scene likely to be confusing to readers not familiar with the processes for sharing official scores at Bethany's school. The capitalized material following Bethany's topic sentence in that paragraph captured the questions I had raised with Bethany during our discussion:

We went back to our seats and exchanged our scores with everyone. WERE YOU SUPPOSED TO? WHAT WERE TEACHERS DOING AT THIS POINT? DID ANYONE ACKNOWLEDGE THE SCORE SHARING? WAS IT SUPPOSED TO HAPPEN AT THIS TIME?

Since Bethany had not addressed any of the questions yet, Janice wrote her a note asking her to do so and bumped her to a later slot on her conference plan. Janice was then able to confer with another student in more need of adult support during the first part of the composing block. This move promoted more independence on Bethany's part at the same time it allocated the precious resource of adult time and attention more efficiently.

Finally, embedded notes helped staff work together to support ongoing revisions across multiple composing sessions. An early instance of this took place in Year 2, when Jake and I alternated conferring with Ismail, a US-born Black boy who was writing about an altercation in his neighborhood. Jake and I agreed that Ismail's action scenes were some of the most vivid we had ever seen from a writer of his age, but his poor control of conventions associated with formatting and punctuating complete sentences was significantly reducing readability. Our conferences focused on helping him to eliminate most of his run-on sentences to improve clarity while acknowledging that some of those run-ons were extremely effective in conveying the confusion and unpredictability of the moment in real time. We focused on teaching Ismail to be intentional about whether a run-on sentence was serving his purposes or whether it should be divided into separate sentences with capital letters and end punctuation. Because the first draft of the text was so lengthy, we chunked it into parts for editing and used embedded notes to indicate which sections had been reviewed with an adult, which needed Ismail's independent editing in a given composing period, and which needed attention at another time. The plan helped Ismail sustain focus on what might otherwise have been a daunting editing task, despite his considerable investment in the piece. The notes also helped Jake and me coordinate our efforts, allowing either of us to confer with Ismail quickly between other students.

Conferring is, by design, an individualized, often improvisational, instructional approach. It was central to institute staff members' ability to address the varying, sometimes idiosyncratic needs of our heterogeneous group. (Most attendees would neither have benefited from nor appreciated the sentence-level work Jake and I did with Ismail had we attempted lessons with that focus in the LGIR.) At the same time, our use of shared tools and routines such as the strengths-first protocol, record-keeping forms, and embedded notes helped us prepare to be more responsive in those individual interactions. Shared planning and debriefing leveraged the wisdom of the collective to support student learning, even when just one teacher was present for the conference.

Tips and Takeaways

Numerous staff members reported drawing on conference-related tenets and tools in their academic-year work with students. Janice recruited the paraprofessional in her inclusive senior English class to be her conferring partner. She shared some open-ended questions to ask in the conferences, showed the paraprofessional how to take notes on a record-keeping form, and assigned her "just six kids to start out with." According to Janice, the colleague was "thrilled," because she wanted "to be a part of the class [and] she has all sorts of things to offer. She spends all day long pushing in to English classrooms. We need to be using her to help benefit kids and . . . build relationships."

As you conduct conferences with student writers in your context, consider the following:

- *Use a protocol for planning and documenting conferences.* An explicit commitment to naming a student's strengths first will build habits that interrupt deficit perspectives. Keeping the protocol simple will increase the chances that you can sustain it on your own and that any collaborators you enlist can use it consistently with minimal training.
- *Track information from conferences with simple and adaptable record-keeping forms.* Schedule time intentionally to review the forms for patterns on your own or with a colleague if you're working collaboratively.
- *Share drafts of student writing to elicit others' perspectives on productive conferring paths.* Co-teachers and colleagues who teach your students in other classes are the most obvious choices, but those who teach at the same grade level or assign similar kinds of writing may also be willing to share their insights. Focusing your plans on identifying one strength and one teaching point will reduce the time needed for such interactions, increasing their appeal for busy people.
- *Enlist additional help during intensive conferring periods with focal genres.* Using big-picture planning tools like the fifteen-day organizer described in chapter 2 will help you identify in advance when this extra help will be needed. Possible categories of people to draft might include:
  - other teachers or paraprofessionals who share your students, including teachers of special education and English as a new language
  - your building's library media specialist (especially if the writing involves research and/or technology use)
  - building administrators
  - recently retired educators (like Mary Taylor)
  - pre-service teacher candidates
  - community volunteers (including those you might recruit as guest writers)
- *Show those you enlist how to use your record-keeping forms and schedule time to discuss their interactions with your students over those notes.* Such debriefing will enhance their experience, improve their effectiveness with youth, and elicit ideas from them that can inform your next steps.

CHAPTER 7

Supporting Student Collaboration

It's Thursday, Day 9 of Year 4, and the first slide in the opening meeting PowerPoint presentation includes this question: "Who helped someone else, and how, yesterday?" The question continues a conversation from the previous day, when I told students about city councilor Nader Maroun's visit to the institute several years before. Maroun had invited those participants to make eye contact with peers sitting to the left and right of themselves and then charged them to help one another "get where they need to go" over the next four years. His positive, community-oriented request directly contrasted with the weed-out language (e.g., "by the time you graduate, one of you will be gone") common in media depictions of launch ceremonies for high school students, military cadets, or police academy trainees. When I described this moment, which I called "Mr. Maroun's challenge," to the Year 4 group, I asked them to find opportunities throughout the Wednesday session to give and receive help as writers. I promised that the next opening meeting would include some time to give credit where it was due.

Now when I open the floor for volunteers to report on what they have tracked, half a dozen contribute immediately. Kiara says she received title ideas from two people. Winton describes the proofreading help he received from a friend. Rebecca, a staff member returning for a second year, compliments two students for encouraging each other in the computer lab. Some of the examples are rooted in relationships that predate the program and reflect shared identity by gender or first language. Other assistance has flowed from student to student less predictably, in ways grounded in common experience within the institute. It is clear that students are sensitized to the roles that peers have played in their writing process and that the program's daily routine has offered multiple opportunities to support one another.

I open with this scene because it demonstrates our team's commitment to framing peers as essential resources in individuals' writing development and building community within the institute. It shows that concern for such collaboration among students, not just among teachers as I detailed in chapter 2, was an important program component—one refined across multiple iterations. After providing some background about how our design drew on the literature on writing and collaboration, I organize the chapter into two sections. In the first I share how we supported students' interaction around their writing. In the second I focus on design choices we made to promote their collaborative composing, with a particular focus on digital stories.

Why We Embraced Student Collaboration

For many years conventional wisdom has positioned writing as a solitary, often silent endeavor. Television and film are replete with examples of reclusive individuals, often male, who fuel themselves with coffee and retreat from the world to type or scribble page after page of text. Recent research has revealed this archetype to be an inaccurate representation of writing in many contemporary workplaces, community organizations, and affinity groups, particularly those influenced by digital technologies.[1] In these contexts writing can be intensely social, requiring groups and teams to construct meaning with complex multimodal texts ranging from film scripts and fan fiction to basketball plays and marketing plans.[2] Even when contemporary writers publish the kinds of books that historically feature one name on the cover—literary novels, for instance—their often lengthy acknowledgments reveal the influence of social interaction on how such texts are researched, drafted, revised, and disseminated.

Many schools in the US, however, still frame writing as an independent undertaking. This trend is reinforced, in no small part, by the influence of standardized tests in the past two decades—tests that assess solitary, unassisted composition, typically in print genres.[3] To prepare students for such composition, which can have high stakes for student promotion, teacher compensation, and even school closures, teachers offer direct instruction and repeated practice with tasks that parallel the testing expectations, despite evidence that such practices achieve limited results.[4] Because the ability to collaborate on writing is not tested, it is often not taught.

That said, research evidence suggests that social interaction around writing can improve performance. The *Writing Next* report cited collaborative writing, defined as "arrangements in which adolescents work together to plan, draft, revise, and edit their compositions," as a highly effective feature of writing instruction.[5] Collaborative writing was, in fact, the element with the third largest effect size (.75) of the eleven elements reviewed. Other studies have shown that peer collaboration can increase motivation to compose, promote awareness of audience, offer alternative approaches to planning, and help students access specialized practices associated with a particular discipline.[6] These findings hint at significant payoff for teachers who orchestrate collaborative activities successfully in their classrooms.

As I began my partnership-focused work at Robinson, ideas about writing, collaboration, and diversity were intersecting for me. At the time, my colleague Paula Kluth and I were completing a line of inquiry focused on supporting the literacy development of students with autism.[7] Our findings suggested that the presence of students on the autism spectrum in inclusive classrooms might have literacy benefits for all students, not just those with that particular disability label. We argued that teachers who see heterogeneous learning communities as an asset to learning, not a liability, are well positioned to expand conceptions of literacy and value multiple ways of participating in classroom life. This potential is especially high in contexts where teachers engage their students in devising meaningful ways for everyone to connect. With this work as a backdrop, maximizing social interaction among writers with diverse needs became a key node of the guidance document for the Robinson PD. I placed particular emphasis on peers with varying profiles supporting each other in early phases of the writing process and on serving as an authentic audience for finished work.

The Year 1 staff for the institute took up these ideas readily, possibly because many were already circulating in the Brown district. At the time, I knew numerous teachers in Brown's middle and high schools who were working to link reading, writing, and peer talk more closely in their English instruction. In addition, Robinson offered multiple extracurricular activities and electives, including a popular class on culture and social justice taught by Rebecca, that brought diverse groups of youth together around shared interests. These efforts to promote collaboration across a heterogeneous student body were blunted, however, by tracking practices that reduced interaction among some student populations and, in some instances, led to de facto segregation by race, language, and disability status. Collaboration opportunities were also reduced by the district's adoption of a computer-based, commercial literacy intervention in low-track ninth-grade classes that put headphones and screens between students and their peers (and concomitantly reduced access to computers for composing, research, and multimedia design).

Our team's design for the institute was thus intended to offer an alternative vision for addressing student writers' diverse needs. This inclusive vision resisted ability grouping and valued face-to-face exchanges among individuals even when—perhaps *particularly* when— they composed with technology. We contended that collaborative skills and strategies were no different from any other aspect of literacy: they needed to be taught deliberately and explicitly to ensure access for all learners, not just those from the backgrounds historically best served by schools.

Supporting Peer Interaction around Writing

In the institute we took British scholar James Britton's famous assertion that "writing floats on a sea of talk" as an informal motto.[8] We discussed it among ourselves, and we shared it with the students on a PowerPoint slide in opening meeting, accompanied by a picture of a message in a bottle bobbing among the waves. The moves we made to enact that motto included planned seating, flexible grouping, and scaffolded interactions. As with other aspects of the program, these elements were designed collaboratively and iteratively during afternoon planning and then enacted by staff co-teaching in varied configurations.

Seating

Beginning in Year 1 we prioritized planned seating in whole-program spaces to help us learn students' names and build relationships quickly within the compressed time frame. We wanted students to feel known and appreciated as individuals so that they would trust us enough to take risks as writers. Because students came from multiple middle schools, they needed to get to know each other swiftly as well. Consequently, for the first two days of the program, when we had limited student information, we assigned seats alphabetically in the LGIR, which featured two permanent clusters of rows, with aisles in the middle and on each side. Each staff member had a copy of the seating chart on which to take observational notes, and we used those notes, plus data from initial student surveys, to inform seating adjustments we unveiled on Day 3.

Those adjustments were intended to serve varied purposes. Jarrick, a student with autism who carried multiple dictionaries as comfort objects and whose legs were very long, benefited from an aisle seat where he could extend himself and his belongings. Kaid, a recent arrival from Iraq whose English was very emergent, was better off in the front row, where staff co-facilitating instruction could spot nonverbal cues when he was confused. Just as many teachers do during the school year, we separated students who distracted each other or had visible conflicts with one another. By pooling data across the team, we surfaced a lot of differentiation concerns that adjustments to the seating chart could help address.

Even more powerful (as we came to realize after repeating the process in Years 3 and 4) was the fact that discussions about the seating chart prompted by *some* students' specific needs catalyzed us in thinking more carefully about the affordances of seating for *all* students. The seating chart wasn't just about managing behavior or offering modifications; it was an important tool in supporting varied peer interactions around writing. We began to conceptualize each student in space—to consider the talk possibilities offered by peers seated in front of or behind particular students, not just beside them in a row. This perspective allowed us to position English language learners near a peer who spoke the same first language whenever possible so that the two could draw on that shared linguistic resource. At the same time, we could ensure proximity to native English speakers in other directions in order to offer monolingual and multilingual students opportunities to learn from one another. When we considered the seating chart holistically, we shifted from heading off particular problems for a handful of students to supporting the exchange of texts and ideas for the entire cohort.

Careful construction of the revised chart was then accompanied by whole-team conversation during afternoon planning about how to use it in opening or closing meeting. We could ask students to combine in pairs, trios, or quads, depending on whether individual airtime or consideration of multiple perspectives was more valuable for the task. We could make quick groupings with a gesture and a word or two— two fingers held aloft, for instance, signaled groups of two; a circling gesture meant that the last two students to receive eye contact from the staff member were assigned to each other. If time was running short, the facilitator could deliver an efficient directive to "talk about your current title idea for two minutes to the person in the row behind you." Occasionally we invited students to select talk partners themselves, but even then our instructions emphasized the community: "If you can, pick someone you haven't talked to much lately . . . and look around you to make sure no one gets left out."

In instructional spaces led by dyads, where the group sizes were smaller, staff made more flexible seating decisions, often after quick consultations with one another. Even in these spaces, though, we sometimes found reasons to assign seating. As students neared the completion of their personal narratives, for example, we used sticky notes with names on them to direct students to specific computers in the labs. Sometimes we sought to prevent the one student trying to evade teacher scrutiny from sitting at the one machine not easily accessible to an adult supervising the room. More often, though, we wanted to seat students with similar instructional profiles—for example, a need to make their "So what" more explicit to the reader—close to each other so that we could confer efficiently with more than one at a time.

The role of seating in creating an inclusive community ethos was best revealed by two data sources. One was staff observation during Year 4, when a communication snafu interfered with the preparation of the alphabetical seating chart and led to self-selected seating on Day 1. As Crystal noted later during afternoon planning, students' congregating with peers they already knew led to clusters from the two largest-sending middle schools sitting on opposite sides of the room, with nearly all of the White enrollees together in one area. (Perhaps needless to say, we made sure to have a seating chart to interrupt this pattern for Day 2.) The protocol breach underscored the idea that students were not likely to venture out of their interactional comfort zones on their own, at least not right away. The second data source—exit surveys from students with varying profiles—suggested that many kids knew this and could identify the interactional benefits of assigned seating. Philippa from Year 2 noted that a program highlight for her was "sitting next to people who are now friends." Sahra from Year 4 wrote that she liked "when we got assigned seats because I met some really cool people. If we had not had assigned seats we would have just sat with our friends and not met new people." Both came into the program with well-established peer networks, and neither would likely have been the focus of much attention in a seating process focused on addressing the most obvious student needs. Our expanded vision for seating, however, increased their access to new ideas and new peer relationships.

Grouping

Flexible grouping was another tool we used to maximize social interaction among peers. We wanted to challenge assumptions about student capacity (or lack thereof) that were constructed and reinforced by daily practices during the academic year, such as Lexile-driven reading groups and pull-out special education services. As recommended by James Flood and his colleagues in a now classic article,[9] we varied group size and composition depending on instructional purpose, typically with an eye toward maximizing diversity and inclusion.

Early in the program, as discussed in chapter 3, we divided youth participants into two or three heterogeneous groups, depending on enrollment, assigned to work most closely during the first half of the program with one teaching team. During the last frenetic day or two, when the crunch was on to ensure screenable products for all, we "triaged" digital story groups, assigning some to teachers who were familiar with the bells and whistles of Photo Story 3, some to teachers experienced with audiotaping narration, and still others to teachers skilled at midwifing scripts at the last minute. (This last category of groups earned the affectionate appellation of the "hot messes" in Year 1, which stuck.) Across the three weeks, students would experience half a dozen different configurations, as summarized in table 7.1.

Aside from the dyad groupings, the most persistent—and perhaps most important—of the configurations were pairs and trios for digital stories. We launched this process with several brainstorming sessions to generate topics of interest, with the adapted "deciding what to say" activity described in chapter 4 chief among them. Students noted their top three topic choices on index cards, in order of preference, which we summarized on the whiteboard during afternoon planning, usually around Day 8 or 9. Each student's name was recorded under multiple topic headings so that we could see more than one option for placement.

TABLE 7.1 Overview of typical groupings

Type	Size	Employed When	Mechanism
Focal genre rotations	One-third of program enrollment	Day 2	Randomly assigned
Dyad group	One-third of program enrollment	Day 3 to program end	Teacher-selected, using observational data and baseline writing samples from Days 1 and 2 to maximize heterogeneity
Digital story group	Pairs and trios of students	Around Day 7 to program end	Teacher-assigned, with student input on topics
"Triage" groups	Variable, depending on need	Day 12 or 13	Teacher-assigned
Elbow partnerships to share ideas and/ or drafts	Pairs of students	Various throughout program	Sometimes teacher-assigned, sometimes self-selected

Once a viable group was formed, we circled the names assigned to it and eliminated those names wherever else they appeared, as the photograph in figure 7.1 depicts. Topics such as poetry or songwriting often attracted considerable interest, allowing us to create more than one grouping with that focus. When this process was complete, typically yielding twelve to eighteen groups, we divided those groups evenly among the teaching teams, separating groups with similar topics to offer multiple vantage points on the essential questions while maximizing students' opportunities to work closely with new pairs of teachers.

Topical interest was not the only grouping consideration, however. In Year 2, for example, we took care to ensure that Jarrick, the student with autism, whose fascinations included dictionaries and vocabulary, had appropriate partners. On his index card, he expressed interest in exploring different writing systems in history—a topic that no one else identified as compelling. Staff discussion during planning led to a solution, though: we grouped Jarrick with two peers who demonstrated patience and interpersonal skills but struggled to articulate an inquiry focus of their own. (One of their index cards noted very broad interests; the other

FIGURE 7.1   Emerging groupings for digital stories

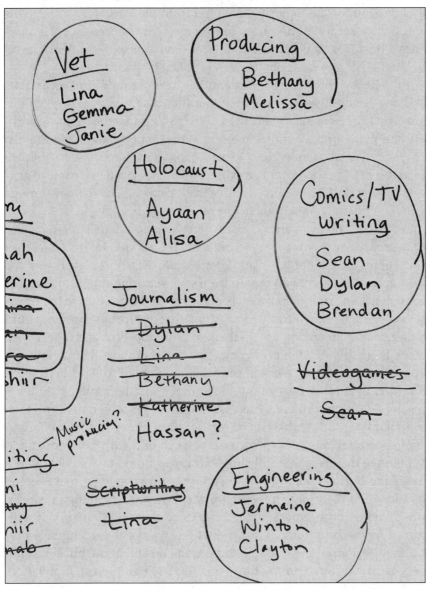

was incomplete.) They benefited from Jarrick's background knowledge and passion for the topic; he benefited from their organizational skills and their insertion of humor to leaven the script and engage the audience. ("Just in case you live under a rock, an alphabet is a standard set of letters that represent phonemes in spoken language.")

Proficiency with English was another important grouping variable, and our perspectives on how to account for it shifted over time.[10] During Year 1 we were most concerned with making sure that English learners had many opportunities to interact informally with native English speakers. We also tended to construct trios to include students that we assessed in a traditional high, medium, low schema when it came to general writing skill. The combination of these priorities led to many groups with one ELL assigned to them but rarely more than one.

In Year 2, however, an increased percentage of English learners and more sharply articulated topic interests for all kids led us to rethink some of these assumptions. Valerie and Akila, the tennis players profiled in chapter 3, served as an important test case during our grouping discussions. Some staff members were concerned that neither of them was strong enough academically to "anchor" that group and that we should either split them up and assign them to other topics or add a peer with more English language proficiency for more support. Ultimately our appreciation for their passion prevailed; we opted to pair them without forcing another peer to pursue a topic of limited interest, and we resolved to support them as necessary via teacher conferences. We took a similar approach with a trio of African-born girls with a shared interest in personal journals. That group worked diligently to conduct and synthesize their research, enlisting extra help from Mary Taylor, whose modeling during opening meeting about her own avid journal keeping had inspired their idea in the first place. When the final digital stories produced by both groups turned out to be quite high quality, it reinforced the need to think in less reductionist ways about language proficiency as a grouping variable. It needed consideration, but it did not necessarily need to trump other variables such as interest, motivation, and work ethic.

Scaffolding Peer Interactions

Thoughtful seating and grouping patterns were necessary but not sufficient for supporting productive peer interactions around writing. To acknowledge and leverage the varied learner profiles within our population, we had to design other instructional scaffolds. Helping students to establish a public voice and presence within the program was foundational to these efforts. Early on in Year 1, for example, the full staff adopted a phrase—"Loud and proud to rock the crowd"—that Mary, a Brown district veteran for more than thirty years, used when students spoke inaudibly while sharing an idea or reading their writing. We explained to the kids that developing a strong voice in these contexts was related to college readiness, and we avoided teacher revoicing as much as possible for this reason. Other small but significant moves intended to establish and amplify student voices in the program included the following:

- recording individual student contributions publicly on chart paper or the whiteboard
- praising students for staying on task for the full allotted time for peer discussion
- noting good ideas that emerged during peer discussion and nudging their originators to share those thoughts with the whole group
- inviting students to choose their preferred community appreciation (e.g., clapping, snapping, finger waves) when they shared writing in progress

In addition to encouraging individuals to share their own ideas, we deliberately designed instruction to support careful attention to—and faithful representation of—others' perspectives. During one discussion of a personal narrative exemplar in Year 4, for instance, we asked students to confer with an "elbow partner" before the whole-program discussion. Billy and Jake, who were co-leading the meeting, opened the floor first for individuals to share an idea they heard from their partner, not one of their own, with attribution. When Jermaine took up this invitation with particular detail and precision, Billy directed the crowd to give him two snaps, an appreciation most associated in the program with bravely sharing a draft text. That move was intended to signal the high value we placed on listening to and crediting each other for good ideas.

Another example of a lesson structured to promote peer talk took place during the Day 7 opening meeting in Year 3. The focus was on sharpening the "So what" of students' personal narratives. We began with a warm-up prompt to get participants reflecting on how clearly the point of their narrative was coming through in their current draft:

Write a paragraph or two about your personal narrative answering one or more of these questions:

- Why does this story matter? Why tell it?
- What did you learn from it?
- What does it show about you as a person?

Once students were primed to think about their "So what," Paul and Lorraine, the graduate student interns on our staff that year, directed them to create a chart in their notebooks with columns for title, topic, and so what. (By separating each of these constructs from each other, we hoped to address a pattern we were seeing that had many students conflating the literal topic of their narrative with its point.) The first three rows of the chart pertained to exemplar texts from past cohorts that current participants had already read and discussed from other perspectives. Paul and Lorraine led students through exploration of those common texts, first eliciting ideas from the whole group about Dayton's Year 2 story focused on getting fitted for contacts and then inviting students to pair with a neighbor to discuss and record ideas about Seth's Year 1 narrative about losing the family dog.

Later in the day, in dyad groups, teachers reset consideration of the chart by modeling how to reread their own narratives to identify places where they could cut or add material to make the message more salient. Students then worked with a new partner to use this same process with their respective drafts, culminating in the recording of two more lines— one for their own draft, one for the peer's text—in the three-column chart. (See figure 7.2 for an example from Vanessa.) Through this sequence of activities, youth participants considered the "So what" construct across five other narratives, plus their own, and engaged in structured, sustained discussion with two different peers. The combination of large- and small-group talk gave them multiple opportunities to process the content and consider its implications for their own writing.

Before I conclude this section, it's important to note that peer conferences of this type—those focused on the content, organization, and language choices in another participant's draft—were common across all four iterations of the program. Peer conferences about conventions— mechanics, grammar, and spelling—were less so, by design. As a staff we shared the belief that all students could identify parts of a piece that were working well or ask questions about sections that were confusing.

FIGURE 7.2 Vanessa's "So what" chart

Title	Topic	So What	7/17/12
Tooth Fairy Trickery	losing a tooth	Families sometimes torture each other but still love each other	
Contacts	A boy replacing his glasses with contacts.	• Contacts make life easier— you don't get teased • when something is wrong, you should tell someone	
Dog Story	Family loses their dog	• Moving on might be the best way to get over loss.	
Leaving	Leaving Nigeria	• Leaving a place is hard but you can choose to be happy and sad, both.	

Interacting over a draft with a peer who did not share one's linguistic or cultural experience could be especially helpful, as it often identified gaps that readers with similar backgrounds might not have apprehended. When it came to technical details, however, most of us agreed with veteran English teacher Kelly Gallagher's assertion that most adolescents edit each other's work poorly, with some going so far as to introduce new errors into conventional text.[11] Unless we had taught a conventions-focused lesson needing follow-up (e.g., an annual session on formatting dialogue that was necessary given its prevalence in students' personal narratives), we tended not to use much peer editing.

Our initial instincts that peer editing would not serve us well were validated during Day 14 of Year 1 when a few students who considered their personal narratives and digital stories "done" (their words, not ours) asked us if they could edit for other students. Such a request seemed like the logical extension of our emphasis on social interaction around writing throughout the program, and staff were stretched with helping all groups complete their digital stories in time to screen them at the celebration. Having more hands on deck seemed like a good idea. When we debriefed on the events of the day later, however, we realized that the students making the requests to peer edit were nearly all White, English-speaking girls without disability labels from the sending school with the highest percentage of middle-class professional families. The homogeneity of their profiles hinted at their relative privilege within the program and, likely, within the instructional spaces they had inhabited previously. Designating them as roving peer editors might have supported their leadership development, and it might have produced better edited texts for the peers they assisted, but it positioned some participants as "helpers" and others as "the helped" in potentially racialized, gendered, and ableist ways that were inconsistent with the inclusive ethos of our community. To interrupt that pattern and occupy those who finished their focal genres early, we developed the list of extension tasks that appears in figure 7.3. It did not include peer editing as an option.

Supporting Collaborative Composing

Because the institute was situated within a larger early college initiative, we took a future-oriented stance whenever we could. It was not enough to write well for the moment—to achieve a satisfactory grade from a current teacher. Instead, we wanted students to be aware of how

FIGURE 7.3   Extension tasks for the last workday

If you are finished with both your personal narrative and your digital story, do one or more of the following:

___ Copy and paste the text from your personal narrative or digital story script into www.wordle.net and print the graphic it creates to display at tomorrow's celebration.

___ Make a new eight-panel comic reflecting on your digital story process.

___ Add comments to the graffiti charts for guest writers.

___ Sign the thank-you cards for guest writers.

developing new skills and habits of mind would benefit their longer-term success with college, career readiness, and community participation. The ability to compose collaboratively with multimedia tools was central to that success. Over time we conveyed that message more strongly with the digital story topics we chose to model and with a roster of guest writers that included individuals involved in media, entertainment, and marketing, where multimodal composing in teams is common.

We also learned to share our rationales and expectations for collaboration more explicitly with youth participants. One example of this shift comes from our annual announcement of the digital story groupings we painstakingly constructed during afternoon planning. As experienced teachers, we knew that such an announcement could undermine the community if students complained publicly about the peers to whom they were assigned, so our collective plan for that day in Year 1 allocated time to address that issue: "Go over our expectations for how they will work together in productive digital story groups (9:30–9:35 a.m.)." But the paucity of detail in that portion of the plan reflects our lack of consensus about how to communicate those expectations with something other than a behavioral warning. (And, perhaps not surprisingly, a small but noticeable minority of participants in that first cohort ignored our warning and made their displeasure about their group mates known.)

Keen to avoid a repeat of this moment, we worked in each successive year to refine the message about our group expectations. By Year 4 that segment of our plan, co-facilitated by Sue and Crystal, still took five minutes, but it was much more detailed, with positively framed language to explain our decision-making:

Talk about our expectations for how they will work together in productive digital story groups:

- Compliment them first on what a cooperative, respectful group they have been in general.
- Say that we made digital story groupings primarily around topics, though we also thought about who would work well together—who would stretch each other, who would support each other.
- Make it clear that everyone will work in a group with at least one other person, that these are part of the skills we're trying to develop that lead to high school success.
- Share our unanimity about how much we, as teachers, appreciate students who are open to working with a wide range of peers, that we would rather have a C student who is cheerful about this in our classes, including our college classes, than an A student who sucks their teeth, rolls their eyes, or says nasty things—either publicly or under their breath—about the peers to whom they are assigned.
- Tell them we expect them to show us their best selves later today when they are assigned to their groups (9:55–10:00 a.m.).

When the topics and members for fifteen digital story groups were displayed, not a single student signaled dissent. They opened up their writer's notebooks at Crystal's cue and matter-of-factly began to list what they knew about their assigned topics, as a precursor to meeting with their partners for the first time.

Once the groupings for digital stories were in place, we worked to build students' collaborative writing capacities. Key to these efforts was an adaptation of the noticings routine discussed in chapter 3. When we used this approach with text exemplars in the focal genres, we asked students to attend to key text features that they might reproduce in their own writing. When we adapted it for interactional models, we asked students to attend to the collaborators' processes for insights about how they might work with one another.

From Year 1 on, our first use of this routine was applied to the same short video, a documentary of the making of pop musician Rob Thomas's single "Streetcorner Symphony" with guest John Mayer sitting in on guitar.[12] In the studio footage, Thomas and Mayer negotiate with each other and with several other musicians and producers while snippets of their talk are layered over the finished song. The video, which we usually showed and discussed during a closing meeting to set the tone for group work in the subsequent day, appealed to us because it modeled healthy collaboration that was multimodal, not just print-based, and took place outside of an academic context. As they watched, students recorded observations in their writer's notebooks about what they saw and heard the collaborators do. A pair of teachers then led a whole-program debriefing discussion, recording ideas from students in a projected document that everyone could see.

Figure 7.4 reproduces that document from the Year 4 conversation led by Janice and me. The notes reveal that students recognized numerous components of successful group composing, including collective idea generation, clarification strategies, and openness to compromise. The notes also offered evidence of the success of our attempts, detailed in the previous section, to invite a wider range of students into public discourse. Of the ten ideas on the list, seven were from students who had not contributed during opening meeting the same day, with three coming from kids who had not previously shared an idea during whole-program discussion at all. Janice named these patterns explicitly, praising the previously reticent students for being intrepid enough to share and our more regular contributors for holding back a bit to allow new

FIGURE 7.4   Group noticings about the "Streetcorner Symphony" video

---

What makes this group's process so successful?

What did they do and say?
- They each gave ideas—different ways to improve.
- They met in the middle—they talked about and decided together what was the best choice.
- They were repeating each other's ideas.
- They didn't get frustrated with each other.
- They asked each other questions.
- They planned what they would do.
- They specifically talked about music.
- They elaborated on each other.
- They communicated well with each other.
- They gave each other advice.

---

voices to be heard. She then reminded students to employ some of the important strategies they had identified when their own collaborative groups next met.

Shortly after the "Streetcorner Symphony" clip viewing each year, we planned for some teacher modeling of the research process for digital stories. During one iteration, I described how I located old family photos and accessed Alzheimer support websites; during another, Billy explained how he reviewed college memorabilia and informally interviewed a key source. By Year 4, however, we realized that these models were missing a key element: they didn't illuminate how to navigate such tasks when working collaboratively. Our awareness that these skills were difficult for youth participants to master had informed our construction of the graphic organizers and accompanying processes I described in chapter 3, but we had not identified the mismatch between our own process of authoring digital story exemplars as individuals and our expectation that students would do that work in groups.

To address this issue, we devised a plan for Day 10 that called for a pair of teachers to model how to come to consensus on an essential question and devise a preliminary work plan. Rebecca and Sue, who cotaught in a dyad during Year 1 but worked with other partners in Year 4, volunteered to co-lead the meeting. (Later, after it went so smoothly, they confessed that they practiced its delivery while getting pedicures together in the late afternoon—an element of successful co-teaching that I respect but don't recommend as required!) Their proposed digital story focused on the benefits of journaling, with subtopics about famous people who journal and the relationship between journaling and sports to accommodate specific interests for each. They discussed their search strategies and decided on deadlines before asking students to make some notes about what they saw and heard.

When students shared their noticings about the conversation, some ideas surfaced that were similar to the "Streetcorner Symphony" discussion, but others were more specific to the digital story as a focal genre. Lina, for instance, noted that the teachers used their graphic organizer (the same one I discussed in chapter 3) to "set realistic goals" about how they would obtain music and images for one another's consideration. Of particular interest to the kids was how the pair negotiated differences in interest and working style that might have led to conflict, observations that Rebecca validated by saying, "Yes, Mrs. Trudeau [Sue] wants to get the project done, but she won't be pushy about it." She reminded students to use similar processes during the next part of the day, when their groups would meet over their own graphic organizers. As staff circulated to listen in on those meetings later, we heard many partners using language similar to what Sue and Rebecca modeled to propose ideas tentatively, elicit each other's perspectives, and confirm agreement before moving on.

Over the next week, as groups moved more squarely into researching, scripting, and constructing their digital stories, much of our support for students' collaborative composing took place during conferences like those I described in chapter 6. Sometimes these conferences required a very light adult touch. In Year 4, for example, a group of boys was researching a digital story about writing and engineering. Although the topic was of interest to all three, two had just participated in a university-based engineering program that gave them some common prior knowledge and cemented their social bonds. When I joined their group, they were arguing over two formulations of their essential question. Clayton told me they had voted about which version was better and that he and Jermaine (the two who attended the other program) outnumbered Winton, the minority voice. After reviewing both questions, I told them I liked the winning version better, too, because it was more focused on engineers as people who engage in specific writing practices and not quite so general. Before I left, however, I pointed out that voting, while democratic, can leave members feeling disgruntled. I advised them "to look for a time for Winton to win today," and they assured me they would. By the end of the work period, they had a graphic organizer with balanced contributions from each member, accompanied by body language suggesting that all three felt enfranchised. My minimal intervention had kept them from getting stalled, allowing them to manage the rest of the process themselves.

Other groups needed more overt or sustained intervention from staff, including support for the collaborative construction of their scripts, not just the negotiation of their working processes. One example of this trend was a group of three girls from Year 4 who spoke different first languages from each other but who had some common knowledge of Arabic. They were initially interested in exploring how writing gets taught in schools, but we worried that their emerging English proficiency would make this topic difficult to research in a short time. During afternoon planning, Maddie, who taught ESL during the school year, suggested that their dyad teachers might invite them to compare writing in English to writing in Arabic, allowing them to draw on their experiences while still learning something new. The girls found this idea appealing, and they were able to glean some useful information from an accessible website selected and bookmarked in advance for them. But they still needed fairly intensive support from Sue, to whose dyad group they were assigned, over the week of instruction primarily devoted to digital stories. Ever mindful of not "putting words in their mouths" and careful to cross-check her approach with others during afternoon planning, Sue decided to serve as the group's scribe during their drafting of their script, which is reproduced in figure 7.5. Her support freed them up to build on each other's ideas without being stymied by their slow encoding in English. The availability of multiple adults and the presence of more self-directed groups such as Jermaine, Clayton, and Winton in her balanced dyad roster permitted Sue to devote concentrated time to one group regularly, yielding a joint product that they were proud to screen and others were interested to see.

Over four iterations, our team improved our ability to promote collaboration on writing more generally and to support collaborative composing of digital stories more specifically. These improvements were due partly to our stronger commitment to addressing social interaction explicitly in the program and partly to the increased bandwidth for problem solving available to us when we had a more robust fifteen-day organizer, more confidence in our essential questions, and more experience with our focal genres. Insights about collaboration derived from our own co-planning and co-teaching also served as a resource.

One unexpected source of data corroborating our theories about better supporting social interactions around writing over time came from students' two-week reflections. Each year at the close of instruction on Friday, Day 10, we gave participants a multi-panel blank template with these instructions:

- Create a comic strip that shares what happened and what you learned from the first 2 weeks.
- Include both images and written text.
- Be ready to share at the document camera.

As our plans attended more clearly to students' collaborative writing, these themes became more salient in students' comics. In Year 1, for instance, just 24 percent of participants invoked themes such as meeting

FIGURE 7.5   First page of digital story script scribed by Sue

Words	Speaker	Image
Writing is different in every country.	S	Hello in different countries
In the United States we write in English.	H	English writing
Many countries write and speak in Arabic. They are Egypt, Iraq, Libya, and Saudi Arabia.	A	Map
There are many differences between English and Arabic. In Arabic we write in reverse order from English, right to left, and it is in cursive.	H	Arabic writing
In English we write left to right, and the text doesn't have to be cursive.	A	English writing
In the Arabic alphabet there are 28 consonants.	S	Alphabet in Arabic
In the English alphabet there are 21 consonants.	H	Alphabet in English
Writing in more than one language is important if you want to be a part of many things.	S	Writing poem
Knowing Arabic allows us to understand mosque and Islam and the Quran and travel in Arabic countries. Many business people speak Arabic. Arabic is the 5th most commonly spoken native language in the world.	A	Mosque

new people, making new friends, or working together in their images or text. By Year 4, however, more than half of our participants (54 percent) explicitly referred to social themes, and they did so with greater specificity, including phrases such as "cooperating and more cooperating," "sharing our work," and "listening to each other" in their print text and images such as three stick figures sitting in an arc around a table, two obviously wearing head scarves, in their visual content. A quarter of the Year 4 cohort made references to social interaction on two or more panels. (See figure 7.6 for an example from Zaynab.)

FIGURE 7.6   Zaynab's two-week reflection in comic form

The shift in emphasis was striking, particularly since the task instructions—communicated on a PowerPoint slide we reused—remained exactly the same from year to year. That such a high percentage of students documented social interaction as salient during their first two weeks is even more noteworthy given that the most relentlessly collaborative portion of the program—the construction of digital stories in small groups—primarily took place during Week 3, yet to occur when the comics were composed. Nonetheless, students' reflections indicated that they recognized the central place of peer collaboration in the program and saw a clear tie between that feature and their growth as writers.

Tips and Takeaways

In an interview following Year 3, Crystal recounted having Dayton, whose contacts-focused narrative appears in chapter 6, in tenth-grade global studies. When students began a World War I project using Photo Story 3, she told Dayton that she knew he was familiar with the tool from having attended the institute the year before she worked in it. She shared her expectation that he would "take the lead and help people" as the class embarked on the first-time project, an idea that Dayton embraced. As Crystal saw it, his use of the software and his participation in varied social interactions around writing positioned him to "step up" in the academic-year class.

As you work in your own context to develop collaborative competence like Dayton's, consider the following:

- *Use seating charts to offer multiple instructional partners for individuals that maximize diversity of perspective.* Gather data about how the various pairings work and adjust them as needed over time.
- *Create a set of index cards with students' names on them as a tool for flexible grouping in each of your classes.* In the institute, our cards typically included color-coded notes about gender, first language, and sending school, as students tended to self-segregate around these variables if left to their own devices. When tentative groups were laid out using the cards, the color coding often revealed imbalances at a glance, allowing quick adjustments.
- *Use the same cards to aid in selecting students to contribute an idea or read a piece of writing.* The cards helped to interrupt predictable sharing patterns that emerged when we overrelied on the strategy of calling on volunteers. Sometimes just the mention of the card pack was enough to nudge new contributors into the discussion or remind frequent hand-raisers to monitor their airtime.
- *Model with other adults how you want students to interact in terms of text and ideas related to writing.* If you co-teach, plan and rehearse such lessons as part of your regular preparation for class. If you are assigned to lead a class as a solo practitioner, use some of the strategies suggested in chapter 6 to identify potential partners, and add the potential for interactive co-modeling to your recruitment pitch.
- *Create graphic organizers to help students share key ideas from their writing or constructed shared texts with their peers.* In the institute, multicolumn planning tools helped groups to establish a shared vision for their digital stories and to divide responsibilities in ways that led directly to the co-construction of their scripts.

CHAPTER 8

Pulling the Thread Through

I t's afternoon planning on Tuesday, Day 12 of Year 4, and we are gearing up for two days of crunch time before the celebration. Although most students have finished their personal narratives, a few still need to fine-tune, mostly because of absences. As is our habit, I have been designated as the "sweeper" with the lingering narratives: Tomorrow I will steal a few moments to confer with each of those students so that the rest of the staff can concentrate on the digital story push.

Before we move on with our agenda, Janice adds one more name to the conference list. She wants me to help Sahra "pull the thread through" of the thought Sahra had a few days ago about the meaning of her American Barbie doll, which Janice thinks is clearer now but could still be addressed more explicitly at the end. As I make a note about this, Crystal comments that we should have a T-shirt that says, "Pull the thread through," which makes everyone around the table laugh. I write the phrase, which has recurred several times during recent planning sessions, on the whiteboard for emphasis, and Janice points out that it does seem to be the theme for this year.

Later, when I review my notebooks, I realize that this theme—pulling on a connective thread to ensure that ideas are addressed thoroughly and coherently—first surfaced during planning the year before and that the same two staff members, Crystal and Janice, were part of the exchange. Day 6 in Year 3 was particularly rocky, with little forward progress on narratives, lots of distracting side conversations, and growing teacher frustration. Day 7 was almost exactly the opposite, generating composing energy for youth and reassuring the adults. To help us analyze what made one session more productive than the other, I framed our afternoon writing prompt around specifically naming what worked well. Staff members' sharing around the table led to the articulation of an important insight about our work, as captured in this excerpt from my field notes:

> The biggest ah ha was that kids were propelled forward by the focused, sustained instruction we provided. Crystal articulated this first, and then Janice framed it in terms of follow through from large group to small group to one-to-one conferences. I wrote that on the board to emphasize it, and now I'm thinking about the metaphor to explain it as a weaving one—pulling something through and not leaving the thread hanging.

In Year 3 the conversation focused on instructional coherence, on making sure that the various components of the program built on one another in service of our goals for students. Now, in Year 4, the metaphor is being extended to both teaching and writing. As a staff we are concerned with pulling threads across instructional contexts, because we understand that this will, in turn, help youth participants like Sahra pull threads across the focal genres in which they compose. That my collaborators see this theme as a T-shirt-worthy slogan suggests its importance in the design for the program that we refined over considerable time and many discussions.

I chose this scene to open the concluding chapter of this book because the thread-pulling metaphor helped me consider what still needs to be shared about the Robinson writing institute and its past, present, and future impact. I have organized the chapter into three parts. In the first part I explore key themes that cut across the multiple years of the project and serve as binding threads for the book as a whole. In the second I share threads that extend beyond the project, describing several instances when staff and I have applied what we learned from the institute to other work. And in the third section I make some final recommendations about how to pull the thread of your reading experience forward into the fabric of your own life as a teacher, coach, or school leader.

Crosscutting Threads

As I pored through drawers full of data across multiple years of the project, three crosscutting threads, or themes, seemed most salient to me. These included curriculum, collaboration, and community, each of which is discussed next.

Curriculum

The first crosscutting theme from the institute is related to curriculum for teaching writing. In the US our approach to curriculum development and implementation tends to be bifurcated. In under-resourced contexts where students experience what H. Richard Milner IV calls "opportunity gaps,"[1] American policy makers at both the state and local levels often mandate use of externally developed curricula aligned with testing expectations and monitor the fidelity of teachers' implementation. Since it is not uncommon for such curricula to pay limited attention to writing when compared to reading or to frame writing narrowly, as a series of procedural steps to follow, it's not surprising that such moves rarely pay off with writing gains.[2] Where test pressures are less significant, teachers may have more autonomy about which written genres to explore and which instructional approaches to employ. This freedom can come with costs, though: it often requires teachers to construct curriculum with inadequate support, which can lead to burnout for them and a lack of coherence for students.

The Robinson institute suggests the power of a third way. Our collaborative use of big-picture and daily planning tools led to a well-sequenced but permeable writing curriculum that enacted high expectations for a heterogeneous population of participants, including subgroups such as English learners and African American males, who have often been poorly served by writing instruction in schools. The iterative nature of design-based research supported adjustments over time to keep the curriculum fresh and ensure an increasingly better "fit" for kids with varying profiles. Because the staff understood and contributed to the design, they did not reject it as generated by outsiders with limited knowledge of the context. They accepted some constraints on their autonomy and creativity because of clear trade-offs in coherence, instructional quality, and efficiency. There were benefits for students and adults from individual staff members making some, but not all, curricular choices.

The writing institute is far from the first project to demonstrate the potential of negotiated balance between teachers' decision-making freedom and curricular guidelines drawing on the wisdom of a collective. Other examples can be found in case studies of successful, multipronged school reform initiatives in the US and in comparative analysis of countries such as Singapore and Finland that have increased achievement while simultaneously attending to issues of equity.[3] What makes the Robinson institute potentially instructive is its narrower focus on writing—the granular view it offers of one group of professionals' efforts to achieve and enact curricular consensus to guarantee real access, not just lip service, to writing development for a heterogeneous group of learners.

Collaboration

A second and related crosscutting thread of the institute involved collaboration. Working together to design and implement the curriculum discussed above leveraged the full staff's varied perspectives and backgrounds, including differences in academic-year teaching assignments, technology expertise, and comfort level with writing. Each chapter of this book includes at least one example, if not several, where instruction became more responsive to students' varied needs because it was conceived or refined with input from more than one person. The specialized expertise associated with additional certifications such as literacy, English as a new language, and special education informed and enriched our instructional plans, even when individuals with those particular certifications weren't assigned to a particular dyad.

Collaboration in the institute offered another benefit as well: co-planning and co-teaching in shared space appears to have increased accountability for professional learning and risk taking while defusing individual defensiveness and anxiety. Although we were not fully aware of the parallels at the time, our design shared some key characteristics with lesson study, a collaborative approach to instructional improvement common in Japan that some see as central to that country's persistent success on international assessments.[4] When Japanese teachers participating in lesson study host live research lessons with children for colleagues from within (and sometimes beyond) their schools, those lessons are commonly taught by a single teacher. Yet the identification of the problem to be explored, the instructional design, and the language used in debriefing reflect shared responsibility for the lesson by a team of three to eight professionals, not just the teacher who volunteered to implement it in public.

In the institute all staff members had a similar stake in each lesson taught in shared space from having co-planned it, but that was not all. They also deeply understood the focal genres from having produced and discussed those genres themselves in anticipation of the need to model. They could select from a wide range of exemplar texts from having reviewed student work program-wide. When they were called upon to extend a lesson co-taught by others to a new context—for instance, a one-to-one conference or a subsequent opening meeting—they were well positioned to pull those threads through with clarity and confidence.

Community

A third and final crosscutting theme is about community. The literature on teaching writing is very clear that students' written products improve when they are part of a supportive community.[5] Writing requires audience awareness and a willingness to take risks, both of which are facilitated by the sense of belonging palpable in exit-survey comments from institute participants such as Dabira from Year 2: "When we [were] in the LGIR made me feel like I had a big family."[6]

What seems to have received less scholarly attention is the converse—the idea that writing together and sharing that writing can contribute to building supportive learning communities in the first place. In the institute students learned about writing from each other in addition to their teachers, but they also learned about each other from their writing. Their personal narratives and associated prewriting revealed aspects of their histories, their families, and their learning trajectories that might otherwise have been unknown to their peers (or the staff). Interacting with guest writers and constructing essential question–focused digital stories illuminated in- and out-of-school interests and career aspirations. Our observations and their survey responses offered considerable evidence that many appreciated the chance to expand their knowledge and their peer networks from interacting around writing. What we did *not* see was much evidence to support the necessity of constructing or maintaining school infrastructures that separate groups of students from one another in the name of differentiated writing instruction.

Youth participants in the institute clearly varied in their encoding fluency, motivation to write, willingness to entertain feedback, and persistence with revising. We adjusted how much support, and what kind, we offered them accordingly. But none of those differences suggested it would be helpful to track them—quite the opposite, in fact. Our dyad and triad groups worked most effectively when they included a balanced mix of strengths and needs, and our instruction was most robust when we sought to account for all students' growth, not just those likely to have qualified for formal academic-year interventions. Our work over four years suggests that educators in middle and high schools concerned with boosting writing achievement—not to mention stronger connections in school—might be better off to prioritize building and supporting heterogeneous learning communities than to invest time and energy in testing, labeling, and sorting students. We have our best chance to achieve this ambitious goal if we strengthen the adult community of learners simultaneously.

Threads That Extend Beyond the Program

In previous chapters I shared numerous accounts from individual staff members about how they applied their learning in the institute to writing instruction in their classrooms during the school year. These examples ranged from Cynthia's inviting students to leave sticky notes in her own writer's notebook to Jake's embrace of modeling, from Janice's recruitment of her teaching assistant to conduct conferences to Crystal's adoption of a digital story project in global history. In this section I describe threads extending beyond the institute that involved collaborations among staff members, including myself, not just individual practice. Two of these initiatives took place at Robinson, while two others seeded new summer programs to benefit youth and adults in new teaching and learning contexts elsewhere.

Threads at Robinson

One significant thread beyond the institute was associated with a six-month period I spent in residence at Robinson between Years 2 and 3. My purpose for this sabbatical was to test the usefulness for academic-year English instruction of (1) the high-utility approaches we used with youth in the institute, including writer's notebooks, think-alouds, conferences, and the like, and (2) the collaborative model we used as adults to generate curriculum and construct collective daily plans. Jake was gracious (and curious) enough to invite me to co-teach with him, and together we selected his third-block class as the best site for our joint work. This group was comprised of seventeen students—including four alumni of the Year 2 institute—who had been assigned to a middle level in Robinson's tracking system, between the advanced class and the computer-based remediation for students seen as most at risk of failing the state test. The class met daily for eighty minutes for the entire year. During the first semester, Jake implemented a strategic reading program intended to accelerate students' literacy progress.[7] During the second semester, when I arrived, we used the big-picture planning process outlined in chapter 2 to put a writing-intensive spin on the district's ninth-grade English curriculum as well as frame it with our own essential questions. We included Caleb, an excellent special educator who pushed into third block every other day, as much as possible in our co-planning, though his time was limited by needing to collaborate with five other Robinson teachers across a two-day rotation. On several occasions we also coordinated with Billy and Sue, both of whom were teaching various levels of ninth grade on other teams in the building.

Our work with Block 3 yielded several successful innovations with roots in the writing institute. We initiated and supported writer's notebooks consistently enough that many students needed a second volume before the end of the school year. We designed an essay assignment that married several strengths of the personal narrative, including scaffolded topic selection and a genuine audience of friends and family, with the new challenge of some preliminary literary analysis. And we offered multiple opportunities for student writers to collaborate with one another, both with regular rounds of peer conferences and with several group projects requiring coauthorship by pairs and trios. As in the summer, these approaches yielded many examples of fine writing from students with varying profiles (although admittedly not as varied as the institute enrollment or Robinson's population at large because of how test scores drove assignment to the class). Perhaps the best indicator of correspondence in our approaches across contexts was that Hadiya, who worked with us in both, complained in exactly the same way about how much writing we asked her to do while revealing with her tone and facial expressions her secret relish at the rigor.

In addition to our in-class experimentation, Jake and I piloted using the after-school Study and Support period—a feature supported by the broader early college initiative—to conduct additional writing conferences with students. (You may recall from chapter 1 that Crystal used that period for similar purposes a year later with her global history students.) By tying attendance at Study and Support to the sanctioning of extended deadlines on major projects, Jake and I enticed a diverse mix of students to attend from all of his classes, including the one with the "advanced" designation, thus challenging easy assumptions about who would benefit. This improved our ability to support and challenge all students, and the resulting heterogeneity of the student population after school improved the overall climate in the space and seeded different kinds of peer-to-peer tutoring and assistance.

Another intriguing outcome of our collaboration was Jake's decision to use some of the materials and instructional routines we developed in the institute, as well as others he and I co-constructed during the semester, with all of his classes, regardless of whether they were designated as advanced or not. Because he had taught more than a dozen of the students on his rosters during the previous summer, he had a good sense of what they were capable of producing, and he wanted to increase expectations for everyone. This move did not dismantle Robinson's well-established tracking system, which still relegated some talented writers like Ahanu to the middle track because of inconsistent grades. But it did introduce what I saw as useful chinks in the rationale for why such a system was ostensibly needed.

A second thread extending beyond the institute involved Sue and Janice. They began co-teaching a twelfth-grade English class after Year 3 of the institute and then were paired as dyad partners the next summer. Their Year 4 professional goals dovetailed with each other's: Sue wanted to get better at working with other adults, while Janice sought to improve her ability to support peers in addressing students' diverse learning needs. Both reported making progress on those goals during the program, and their partnership blossomed even more in subsequent years. Using a combination of text messages, email, and Google Docs, they developed a system for co-planning that preserved the collaborative nature of afternoon sessions in the institute, despite having few formal opportunities to meet during the school day.

Over time Sue and Janice also emerged as teacher leaders in a project headed by several university-based colleagues in inclusive education. The initiative focused on preparing secondary special educators for the complexities of the profession by immersing them in team-based clinical experiences from the very beginning of their programs. Robinson was one of two focal sites for this work, and Sue and Janice were among a core group of school-based personnel who served as mentors and coaches for the preservice candidates. Eventually, they coauthored a chapter about their collaborative processes for an edited volume on differentiating instruction at the secondary level. According to Janice, their writing process for the chapter was "similar to our beautiful mind sessions from the summer." As she explained it: "I am the visual person so I stand at the board and we banter and dictate and make this crazy map" as a way of "writing reflectively about the way we plan." They are currently preparing for their seventh year of co-teaching together and their sixth of working with pre-service teacher candidates.

Threads Beyond Robinson

Two more examples extend the work of the institute to contexts beyond Robinson as a school and Brown as a district. The first involves Bryan Crandall, the doctoral student in English Education who helped to co-design the institute framework and co-directed the program with me in Year 1. After graduating from Syracuse University, Bryan took a job as a professor at Fairfield University that also included serving as director of the Connecticut Writing Project. He immediately began forging writing-focused partnerships across the state but with a particular emphasis on working with teachers and leaders from Bridgeport, an urban school district near Fairfield.

Over the past eight years, Bryan has innovated on the summer writing institute's model to create a series of Young Adult Literacy Labs serving more than two hundred youth each summer, many of whom receive full or partial scholarships, and involving both in-service teachers and university students. He frames his work within the tradition of Ubuntu, a community-based African ethos of "I am, because we are," and takes particular pride in creating opportunities for adults staffing the various one- and two-week initiatives to learn from and with students who identify as refugees and immigrants. The research he conducts in these spaces is both collaborative and formative, just like the Robinson project he helped to launch.[8]

The final example of threads beyond the institute is my own. About six months after the Year 2 program concluded, Janice and I talked about the work she was doing as one of Brown's emerging leaders in special education. At that time the district was sponsoring several professional development initiatives, including peer coaching, and Janice—always curious about others' practice—was participating. She reported learning a great deal from observing and being observed by other colleagues, particularly those with less experience. Despite these benefits, she wondered if a model that featured co-teaching might be more effective than one centered on peer observation: "Walking into classrooms and just sitting and watching someone is not really the same as getting up and being in the trenches and doing it with them."

I pondered Janice's critique for a long time, eventually realizing that it applied not just to Brown's PD but to my own work as well. I was familiar, of course, with long-standing critiques of the gap between campus-based teacher education courses and candidates' fieldwork in K–12 schools.[9] I had conducted collaborative research with school-based partners for years in an effort to close that gap. Ideas from the writing institute infused my methods classes, and students appreciated the currency and concreteness of those examples. Yet it nagged at me that my professional obligations as a teacher educator and the research about which I was most passionate were not more seamlessly aligned. Other people, most notably field supervisors I hired, still observed and assessed my students when they undertook their most important and immersive work in schools: their student teaching placements. If, as Janice noted, sitting and watching wasn't the same as teaching *with* someone, then reading reports from someone else's sitting and watching was even worse.

During the academic year before the Year 4 institute, an idea came into focus with the potential to address this dilemma. Administrators from Leroy, a small high-needs district adjoining Brown, had heard about the early college initiative through professional relationships with Robinson colleagues. A team from Leroy reached out to several faculty from my institution, including me, to gauge our interest in replicating and extending aspects of our work there. It was a propitious moment to make a move, as more than three-quarters of the Robinson English department had staffed the institute in one summer or another, several were poised to take on leadership roles that I typically played, and the external funding that paid for my summer project had run out. With considerable pride and more than a twinge of regret, I decided to step away from Robinson to commence a new, related project at Leroy.

After a year of planning, my Leroy collaborators and I launched Camp Questions, a three-week summer enrichment program focused on literacy and inquiry for students entering grades six through nine. As I write we have just completed our fourth iteration, with no end in sight. The staff includes preservice master's students in secondary education who are taking a required course on literacy across the curriculum. I teach that course—and conduct design-based research on it—with a small team of doctoral students, alumni, and faculty colleagues interested in what Kristien Zenkov and Kristine Pytash call critical, project-based clinical experiences in teacher education, "short-term field experiences with a structure that both supports and is supported by unique school-university partnerships."[10] The teacher candidates work in dyads and triads, with an experienced teacher from Leroy embedded in each group to model practice and coach the novices as they assume increasingly more responsibility over time. (There's that gradual release framework again.) All of us take turns co-teaching in a daily, program-wide opening meeting reminiscent of those in Robinson's LGIR.

Other components adopted or adapted from the writing institute include:

- a strengths-first orientation to interacting with both the Leroy students and the teacher candidates
- a backward-planning process guided by high-level curriculum organizers to balance instructional coherence with responsive daily planning
- extensive use of writer's notebooks by both youth and adults
- adult modeling of their own composing processes
- frequent conferring about written products to take advantage of the generous student-teacher ratio
- flexible grouping of a population that is heterogeneous by skill level, motivation, language status, and (in this new context) age

In addition, we have adopted several practices from Japanese-style lesson study, including two rounds of public lessons for each of the teaching teams and program-wide debriefing, that we see as logical extensions of the Robinson work. Our preliminary analyses suggest that this is generative work for both teacher candidates and experienced teachers.[11]

Like the writing institute, Camp Questions functions as a research laboratory, a service to the community, and a mechanism to maintain the sharpness of my pedagogical tools for working with youth. Unlike the institute, however, I get to do that work side by side with the future teachers who are my own students. For that Robinson-inspired gift, I am grateful.

Pulling Your Own Threads Through

In the preceding chapters, I offered recommendations with the assumption that many readers, though certainly not all, would be concerned with enacting them in their individual classrooms. I made suggestions about reaching out to others, to be sure, but I limited those suggestions to ones that you could most likely execute within middle and high schools as they are traditionally organized, with just a bit of extra effort. In this last section of this final chapter, however, I encourage you to think bigger—to consider how you might collaborate with other colleagues to create new structures or reinvent existing ones to leverage the lessons of the writing institute more significantly. These ideas sit on a continuum of complexity, ranging from replication of a self-contained summer program (which I share first) to reorganization of academic-year schedules to allow for more sustained co-planning and co-teaching (described last).

Offer Summer Enrichment

In the past few years, educators have been increasingly interested in preventing summer literacy loss, the well-documented phenomenon of student skill regression when school is not in session. Programs to promote continuous learning year-round have become common in the school reform tool kit. They represent one strategy for achieving more equitable outcomes for groups historically underserved by school, who also tend to be the same groups most negatively affected by summer loss of learning.[12]

Such initiatives, however, are rarely seen as a strategy for simultaneously building teacher capacity as we did at Robinson. Sometimes they are staffed by individuals who are not employed by the district, a practice that offers students access to diverse perspectives but with limited impact on the quality of the instructional core. In other instances, teachers do staff the program but with parameters that limit their own learning, such as a mandated, scripted curriculum or a dearth of time to plan and review student work. In my view, both scenarios represent missed opportunities for adults' professional growth. Consequently, if your school or district already offers summer enrichment for students, I encourage you to investigate its dimensions and, if needed, to advocate for the redesign or addition of elements that would promote teacher learning about writing pedagogy. If summer enrichment programs for youth do not exist in your context, you and your colleagues might design one, using the blueprint offered in this book as a starting point. My experience—and that of colleagues doing similar work in other locations[13]—suggests that nearby colleges and universities are potential partners with resources to contribute. If they prepare teachers, they may be especially receptive.

Rethink Summer School

Even if your organization doesn't offer summer enrichment to students, there's a good chance it sponsors some kind of summer school. Like enrichment, summer school tends to be discussed in terms of its benefits for students (e.g., staying on track to graduate, experiencing smaller class sizes, etc.). The benefits for adults are centered on earning, not learning, as even the most dedicated professionals in my acquaintance confess that they would pass on summer employment if they did not need the salary supplement. Even for teachers who enjoy being with young people under almost any circumstance, summer school can be what Arlene once described wryly to me in an interview as "soul-sucking."

It could be otherwise, however. It's not difficult to envision an institute-like framework for summer school, where teachers are hired with the expectation of planning and delivering instruction to a shared group of students they combine and recombine flexibly, depending on instructional purpose. The student population might lack some of the heterogeneity of our Robinson cohorts, but I suspect they would still be diverse on many fronts. (Kids fail English or other writing-intensive subjects, such as social studies, for a whole host of reasons, after all, ranging from lack of skill, to boredom, to chronic absenteeism.) The total cost of running the program might increase slightly, given a need to pay teachers for planning time in addition to their contact time with students, but the investment in building teacher capacity would be worth it, particularly if the model also yielded better writing outcomes for potentially vulnerable students, as I believe it would.

Consider Intensive Electives

Another way of pulling the threads of the institute into your school might be to plan a short-term, intensive elective with a focus on writing and collaboration. Although most middle and high schools organize instruction into semester- or yearlong courses, some innovative outliers hint at other possibilities. For example, my colleague Jayne Lammers designed, taught, and researched such an elective with her partner, Judith Van Allstyne, the librarian at an independent school.[14] Ninth through twelfth graders in this context selected several compressed-format electives to take during Maymester, the final three weeks of the school year. Jayne and Judith's course focused on the sharing of fan fiction and creative writing in online communities such as Wattpad, Tumblr, and Fanfiction.net. Students learned about the complexities of cultivating an audience from the experience, while the adults gained valuable insights about supporting and assessing students' progress when much of their composition takes place out of traditional view. As a culminating project, the class jointly constructed a Google site to share insights about writing in online spaces at a schoolwide Maymester Fair.

I can easily imagine a version of the writing institute taking place in this short-term elective format. It's possible that its availability during the school year, rather than amid the competing concerns of summer, might attract a larger or more diverse group of participants than we were able to recruit each July. At Robinson the most convenient timing for such an offering would probably be January, between the first and second semester, when state-level testing for some but not all students already makes the schedule complicated. You likely have a sense of whether colleagues in your context would support the offering of such an elective and where in the cracks and crevices of the school calendar it might fit.

Reconceptualize Co-Planning and Co-Teaching

Most of the productive co-teaching partnerships I've known over my career have been willed into existence by like-minded individuals with unusual drive, persistence, and interpersonal skills. These partnerships often improve learning for the students lucky enough to be enrolled in the target classes, but they rarely have a ripple effect on teaching and learning in the school or district. They're highly dependent on the quality of the relationship between the partners, and they're vulnerable to dissolution with changes in scheduling or responsibilities for one or another partner. The Robinson writing institute was different in that regard. The personal connections that developed across a given year's staff cohort and within each teaching dyad were undoubtedly important. But the co-planning and co-teaching components of the program design transcended the personal preferences or relationship status of particular staff members. As you ponder how to apply these lessons to your own context, I encourage you to think broadly and systematically about how co-planning and co-teaching might support writing instruction for all students.

In my view the more you minimize tracking in your school, the easier it will be for writing-focused collaboration to thrive.[15] Having fewer course levels will permit more balanced diversity within student rosters, reduce teacher preparation time, allow sharing of instructional materials and routines, and increase the number of sections meeting simultaneously that can be combined in varied ways at different times. It will also enhance teachers' opportunities to analyze samples of student writing, both completed and in progress, that are directly relevant to their teaching assignments, even if they were not generated in their own classes.

Once the school schedule has been orchestrated to allow for common planning and common instructional time, you and your colleagues can think flexibly about how, and when, to work together. The institute experience suggests a number of alternatives to putting two teachers in the same class every day, all day. (Such a configuration has many potential benefits but presents clear resource challenges as well.) Numerous classes might combine for presentations by guest writers, allowing you to pool your connections and share the logistical details related to those invitations. Two or more classes might combine in shared space or mix to be redistributed over separate spaces such that one teacher can monitor and manage behavior for independent writing while others conduct individual conferences. Multiple teachers might band together to recruit additional adults for extra support during periods of intensive composing activity. (Think here about my descriptions of the last several days before the institute celebration.) Activities like these will be facilitated by common use of big-picture planning processes and tools like those I profiled in chapter 2. By planning, teaching, and analyzing work samples together in coordinated ways, I predict you will be better able to pull the thread of more equitable and more inclusive writing pedagogy through the contexts that matter most to you.

More About the Students

Pseudonym	Year	Race/Ethnicity	Gender	First Language
Adah	2	Black/African American	Female	English
Ahanu	2	Black/African American	Male	English
Akila	2	Black/African American	Female	Somali
Aliyah	2	Black/African American	Female	English
Andre	1	Black/African American	Male	English
Ayaan	4	Black/African American	Female	Mai Mai
Bashiir	4	Black/African American	Male	Somali
Bethany	4	White	Female	English
Camilla	3	Black/African American	Female	English
Carina	3	White	Female	English
Caroline	3	Black/African American	Female	English
Clayton	4	Black/African American	Male	English
Dabira	2	Black/African American	Female	Mai Mai
Dayton	2	Black/African American	Male	English
Denisha	4	Black/African American	Female	English
Dylan	4	White	Male	English
Eric	2	Multiracial	Male	English
Etan	4	Black/African American	Male	English
Gemma	4	White	Female	English
Hadiya	2	Black/African American	Female	Kiswahili
Hajna	4	Black/African American	Female	Kizigua
Hla	3	Asian American	Female	Karen

Pseudonym	Year	Race/Ethnicity	Gender	First Language
Ibrahim	4	Black/African American	Male	Somali
Imani	4	Black/African American	Female	English
Ismail	2	Black/African American	Male	English
Jadwa	4	Black/African American	Female	Somali
Janie	4	White	Female	English
Jarrick	2	Black/African American	Male	English
Jeremy	1	Black/African American	Male	English
Jermaine	4	Black/African American	Male	English
Jilly	2	Black/African American	Female	Arabic
John	4	White	Male	English
Kaid	2	White	Male	Arabic
Kevin	4	Black/African American	Male	English
Kiara	4	Black/African American	Female	English
Lina	4	Black/African American	Female	English
Luka	1	White	Male	Bosnian
Malik	3	Black/African American	Male	English
Marko	1	White	Male	Bosnian
Marvin	1	Black/African American	Male	English
Marwa	4	White	Female	Arabic
Melissa	4	White	Female	English
Moriah	2	Black/African American	Female	English
Myisha	3	Multiracial	Female	English
Neva	3	Black/African American	Female	English
Nyasia	1	Black/African American	Female	English
Philippa	2	White	Female	English
Rachel	4	Black/African American	Female	English
Sahra	4	Black/African American	Female	Somali
Seth	1	Black/African American	Male	English
Shelley	1	White	Female	English
Tisha	1	Black/African American	Female	English
Valerie	2	Black/African American	Female	Kiswahili
Vanessa	3	White	Female	English
Winton	4	Black/African American	Male	English
Zaynab	4	Black/African American	Female	Kiswahili
Zoya	3	Black/African American	Female	Somali

APPENDIX B

Summer Institute Overview

Italics = Personal Narratives; Boldface = Digital Stories; Roman = Other

	Monday	Tuesday	Wednesday	Thursday	Friday
WEEK 1	Opening meeting: Intros PP of expectations, tasks Three-word activity in notebooks Dyads: Community-building activity with soccer balls Students write about EQs for baseline data Explain independent reading (at least 15 min. for 15 days) then give reading time Closing meeting: Show digital story about writing/ Robinson Index card reflection	Opening meeting: Share wordle, community-building activity around names Dyads: Rotation 1: Writer's notebook decoration Rotation 2: **Show students 2 digital story exemplars from past summers and do writerly noticings;** 15-15 reading Rotation 3: *Writerly noticings about Seth's dog narrative/ teacher think-aloud about how to brainstorm topics for personal narratives [10-10 activity]* Closing meeting: Prepare for Goenka visit, share notebook sample from Jilly	Opening meeting: Guest Tula Goenka [be sure to link back to EQs in debriefing] Dyads: 15-15 reading *Conversation about another PN exemplar Drafting from 10-10 lists Inside-outside circles to share* Closing meeting: Highlight covers and entries from selected students	Opening meeting: *Deciding what to say plus drafting from one idea* Dyads: 15-15 reading *Teacher think-aloud with exemplar text about purpose/so what Students work on committing to topics* Closing meeting: Prepare for Poliquin, mini-lesson on note-taking strategies	Opening meeting: Bud Poliquin Dyads: 15-15 reading Time in computer labs to learn Z drive procedures *Continued drafting of PN in labs; conferring around topic selection/ narrowing* Closing meeting: Reflections on first week, **teacher volunteers share DS**

	Monday	Tuesday	Wednesday	Thursday	Friday
WEEK 2	**Opening meeting: Teacher think-aloud on identifying DS topics & linking to EQs** Dyads: 15–15 reading *Mini-lesson with exemplars on effective beginnings, students try 3 different ways, think-pair-share* **Students write about DS topics then TPS** Closing meeting: Prepare for guests, mini-lesson on note-taking strategies	**Opening meeting: Deciding what to say for DS** Dyads: 15–15 reading *Teacher think-aloud on well-chosen dialogue, using own writing and student samples* *Drafting, revising, and confering* **Closing meeting: Show "Streetcorner Symphony" and talk about group process**	Opening meeting: Guest Katharine Chang Dyads: 15–15 reading *Drafting, revising, and confering* **Closing meeting: Announce DS groups** **Show samples of student planning tools?**	Opening meeting: **Teachers model collaborative process for DS** Dyads: 15–15 reading **Groups have initial meeting over first planning tool** *Drafting, revising, and conferring; mini-lesson about choosing a title?* **Closing meeting: Teacher think-aloud about research/ narration for DS**	Opening meeting: SU student panel Dyads: 15–15 reading *Title revision* **Research time for DS on computers** Closing meeting: 9-panel comics to reflect on 2 weeks

	Monday	Tuesday	Wednesday	Thursday	Friday
WEEK 3	**Opening meeting:** Dyads: 15-15 reading *PN work for stragglers* **Digital story work** Closing meeting: Prepare for guest and reflect on note-taking strategies	**Opening meeting: Song choice workshop** Dyads: 15-15 reading **Digital story work, with regroupings determined by student need** *Polishing of PN, if needed, audiotape snippets for celebration* **Closing meeting: Teacher mini-lesson on writing credits for DS**	**Opening meeting: Teachers model process for audiotaping narration in groups** Dyads: 15-15 reading **Digital story work, with regroupings determined by student need** **Closing meeting: Goal setting for DS groups**	**Opening meeting:** Convene quickly then move to dyads for more work time Dyads: 15-15 reading **Last polish of DS, upload to YouTube; troubleshooting** Closing meeting: Celebration expectations	15-15 reading Writing again in response to EQ, for comparison to baseline writing on Day 1 Final survey/ reflections on participation in Institute Building tour, by dyads Celebration from 10:30–12:00 *Screen DS of PN snippets* **Screen digital stories** Show final video

Product	Instructional Foci
Writer's Notebook (Used throughout program to generate ideas, take notes, draft, etc.)	• Developing fluency • Generating ideas for future writing • Using short bursts of writing to develop more sustained pieces • Taking notes during guest lectures or demonstrations
Personal Narrative (500–750 words, polished, authored independently)	• Finding a satisfying topic • Writing powerful leads • Adding sensory details (but not too many) • Addressing the "So what?" question
Digital Stories (Two to four minutes, authored in groups of two and three, focused on essential questions)	• Using Photo Story 3 and navigating log-in/Z drive, etc. • Using a planning tool integrating attention to narrated text, images, and audio • Connecting personal interests to common essential questions • Rehearsing narration for fluent delivery • Writing credits of various kinds
Overall	• Developing a positive disposition toward revision • Learning to provide specific feedback to others • Learning to use specific feedback from others without getting defensive

Notes

INTRODUCTION

1. As is customary for research, I have used pseudonyms for all teachers and students, as well as for the district and school. University personnel and guest writers are identified by name, as they were not study participants.
2. Kelly Chandler-Olcott and Paula Kluth, "Why Everyone Benefits from Including Students with Autism in Literacy Classrooms," *Reading Teacher* 62, no. 7 (2009): 548–57; Douglas Biklen and Jamie Burke, "Presuming Competence," *Equity and Excellence in Education* 39 (2006): 1–10.
3. David Reinking and Barbara Bradley, *On Formative and Design Experiments: Approaches to Language and Literacy Research* (New York: Teachers College Press, 2008).
4. Jamie Colwell, Sarah Hunt-Barron, and David Reinking, "Obstacles to Developing Digital Literacy on the Internet in Middle School Science Instruction," *Journal of Literacy Research* 45, no. 3 (2013): 295–324.
5. National Assessment of Educational Progress, "The Nation's Report Card: Writing 2011," https://nces.ed.gov/nationsreportcard/pdf/main2011/2012470 .pdf.
6. Paul Gorski, *Reaching and Teaching Students in Poverty: Erasing the Achievement Gap* (New York: Teachers College Press, 2017).
7. Arthur Applebee and Judith Langer, "What Is Happening in the Teaching of Writing?," *English Journal* 98, no. 5 (2009): 18–29; Laurie Henry, "Unpacking Social Inequalities: Lack of Technology Integration May Impede the Development of Multiliteracies among Middle School Students in the United States," in *Technoliteracy, Discourse, and Social Practice: Frameworks and Applications in the Digital Age*, ed. Darren Pullen, Christina Gitsaki, and Margaret Baguley (Hershey, PA: IGI Global, 2009), 55–79.
8. See, for instance, Brad Ermeling and Genevieve Ermeling, *Teaching Better: Igniting and Sustaining Instructional Improvement* (Thousand Oaks, CA: Corwin, 2016).
9. Danny Martinez and Limarys Caraballo, "Sustaining Multingual Literacies in Classrooms and Beyond," *Journal of Adolescent & Adult Literacy* 62, no. 1 (2018):

101–104; Django Paris and Samy Alim, *Culturally Sustaining Pedagogies: Teaching and Learning for Justice in a Changing World* (New York: Teachers College Press, 2017).

10. Biklen and Burke, "Presuming Competence"; Valerie Kinloch, *Harlem on Our Minds: Place, Race, and the Literacies of Urban Youth* (New York: Teachers College Press, 2010); Daniel Gilhooly and Eunbae Lee, "The Role of Digital Literacy Practices on Refugee Resettlement: The Case of Three Karen Brothers," *Journal of Adolescent & Adult Literacy* 57, no. 5 (2014): 387–96.

11. Kelly Chandler-Olcott and Kathleen Hinchman, *Tutoring Adolescent Literacy Learners: A Guide for Volunteers* (New York: Guilford, 2005); Kelly Chandler-Olcott, Helen Doerr, Kathleen Hinchman, and Joanna Masingila, "Bypass, Augment, or Integrate: How Secondary Mathematics Teachers Address the Literacy Demands of Standards-Based Curriculum Materials," *Journal of Literacy Research* 47, no. 4 (2016): 439–72; Kelly Chandler-Olcott and Kathleen Hinchman, "Literacy Co-Teaching with Multi-Level Texts in an Inclusive Middle Grade Humanities Class: A Teacher-Researcher Collaboration," *Journal of Inquiry and Action in Education* 6, no. 3 (2015): 42–63.

12. Kelly Chandler-Olcott, "Using Writer's Notebooks to Support Inquiry and Digital Composing," *Voices from the Middle* 23, no. 2 (2015): 56–61; Kelly Chandler-Olcott and Janine Nieroda, "The Creation and Evolution of a Co-Teaching Community: How Teachers Learned to Address Adolescent English Language Learners' Needs as Writers," *Equity and Excellence in Education* 49, no. 2 (2016): 170–82; Kelly Chandler-Olcott, Janine Nieroda, and Bryan Crandall, "Co-Planning and Co-Teaching in a Summer Writing Institute: A Formative Experiment," *Teaching/Writing: The Journal of Writing Teacher Education* 3, no. 2 (2014), http://scholarworks.wmich.edu/wte/vol3/iss2/3.

CHAPTER 1

1. James E. Rosenbaum and Kelly Iwanaga Becker, "The Early College Challenge: Navigating Disadvantaged Students' Transition to College," *American Educator* (2011): 14–20.

2. The set included these three texts, read in this order: Thomas Newkirk and Richard Kent, *Teaching the Neglected R: Rethinking Writing Instruction in Secondary Classrooms* (Portsmouth, NH: Heinemann, 2007); Lisa Delpit and Joanne Dowdy, *The Skin That We Speak: Thoughts on Language and Culture in the Classroom* (New York: New Press, 2008); and Danling Fu, "*The Trouble Is My English*": *Asian Students and the American Dream* (Portsmouth, NH: Heinemann, 1995).

CHAPTER 2

1. H. Richard Milner IV, "Scripted and Narrowed Curriculum Reform in Urban Schools," *Urban Review* 48, no. 2 (2013): 163–70.

2. Charles M. Payne, *So Much Reform, So Little Change: The Persistence of Failure in Urban Schools* (Cambridge, MA: Harvard Education Press, 2008).

3. Nancie Atwell, *In the Middle: New Understandings about Reading, Writing, and Learning* (Portsmouth, NH: Heinemann, 1998); Penny Kittle, *Write Beside Them: Risk, Voice, and Clarity in High School Writing* (Portsmouth, NH: Heinemann, 2008).

4. Kelly Gallagher, *Write Like This: Teaching Real-World Writing through Modeling and Mentor Texts* (Portland, ME: Stenhouse, 2011).

5. Judith Langer, "Beating the Odds: Teaching Middle and High School Students to Read and Write Well," *American Educational Research Journal* 38, no. 4 (2001): 837–80.

6. Anthony Bryk, Penny Bender Sebring, Elaine Allensworth, Stuart Leppescu, and John Q. Easton, *Organizing Schools for Improvement: Lessons from Chicago* (Chicago: University of Chicago Press, 2010); Heather Zavadsky, *Bringing School Reform to Scale: Five Award-Winning Urban Districts* (Cambridge, MA: Harvard Education Press, 2009).

7. Marc Tucker, *Surpassing Shanghai: An Agenda for American Education Built on the World's Leading Systems* (Cambridge, MA: Harvard Education Press, 2011).

8. Marilyn Friend and Lynne Cook, *Interactions: Collaboration Skills for School Professionals* (Boston: Allyn and Bacon, 2003).

9. Tina Blythe, David Allen, and Barbara Schieffelin Powell, *Looking Together at Student Work*, 2nd ed. (New York: Teachers College Press, 2007).

CHAPTER 3

1. George Hillocks, *Teaching Argument Writing 6–12: Supporting Claims with Relevant Evidence and Clear Reasoning* (Portsmouth, NH: Heinemann, 2011).

2. Arthur Applebee and Judith Langer, *Writing Instruction That Works: Proven Methods for Middle and High School Classrooms* (New York: Teachers College Press, 2013).

3. Joe Onosko and Cheryl Jorgensen, "Inclusive Unit and Lesson Planning in the Inclusive Classroom: Maximizing Learning Opportunities for All Students," in *Restructuring High Schools for All Students: Taking Inclusion to the Next Level*, ed. Cheryl Jorgensen (Baltimore: Paul Brookes, 1998), 76.

4. Kelly Chandler-Olcott, "Seeing All Students as Literate," in *Access to Academics for All Students: Critical Approaches to Inclusive Curriculum, Instruction, and Policy*, ed. Paula Kluth, Diana Straut, and Douglas Biklen (Mahwah, NJ: Erlbaum, 2003), 75.

5. Grant Wiggins and Jay McTighe, *Understanding by Design* (Alexandria, VA: Association for Supervision and Curriculum Development, 2005).

6. P. David Pearson and Margaret Gallagher, "The Instruction of Reading Comprehension," *Contemporary Educational Psychology* 8 (1983): 317–44.

7. Randy Bomer, *Building Adolescent Literacy in Today's English Classrooms* (Portsmouth, NH: Heinemann, 2011).

8. See, for example, Ralph Fletcher and JoAnn Portalupi, *Craft Lessons: Teaching Writing K–8* (York, ME: Stenhouse, 2007); and Katie Wood Ray, *Wondrous Words: Writers and Writing in the Elementary Classroom* (Portsmouth, NH: Heinemann, 1999).
9. Kelly Gallagher, *Write Like This: Teaching Real-World Writing through Modeling and Mentor Texts* (York, ME: Stenhouse, 2012); Nicole Martin and Claire Lambert, "Differentiating Digital Writing Knowledge: The Intersection of Technology, Writing Instruction, and Digital Genre Knowledge," *Journal of Adolescent & Adult Literacy* 59, no. 2 (2015): 217–27.
10. Steve Graham and Dolores Perin, *Writing Next: Effective Strategies to Improve Writing in Middle and High Schools* (New York: Carnegie Corporation, 2007), 5.
11. Lisa C. Miller, "Space to Imagine: Digital Storytelling," in *Teaching the Neglected R: Rethinking Writing Instruction in Secondary Classrooms*, ed. Tom Newkirk and Richard Kent (Portsmouth, NH: Heinemann, 2009), 172–85.
12. The Educational Uses of Digital Storytelling website hosted by the University of Houston can be found at http://digitalstorytelling.coe.uh.edu. StoryCenter can be located at https://www.storycenter.org.

CHAPTER 4

1. Randy Bomer, *Time for Meaning: Crafting Literate Lives in Middle and High School* (Portsmouth, NH: Heinemann, 1995); Lucy Calkins with Shelley Harwayne, *Living between the Lines* (Portsmouth, NH: Heinemann: 1990); Ralph Fletcher, *Breathing In, Breathing Out: Keeping a Writer's Notebook* (Portsmouth, NH: Heinemann, 1996).
2. Aimee Buckner, *Nonfiction Know-How: Strategies for Informational Writing* (York, ME: Stenhouse, 2013); Penny Kittle, *Write Beside Them: Risk, Voice, and Clarity in High School Writing* (Portsmouth, NH: Heinemann, 2009).
3. Steve Graham and Dolores Perin, *Writing Next: Effective Strategies to Improve Writing in Middle and High Schools* (New York: Carnegie Corporation, 2007).
4. Dennis Sumara, *Why Reading Literature in School Still Matters* (New York: Routledge, 2002).
5. Gretchen Bernabei, "The School Essay: Tracking Movement in the Mind," in *Teaching the Neglected "R": Rethinking Writing Instruction in Secondary Classrooms*, ed. Thomas Newkirk and Richard Kent (Portsmouth, NH: Heinemann, 2007), 73–86.
6. Tanya Eckert, B. J. Lovett, B. Rosenthal, J. Jiao, L. Ricci, and A. Truckenmiller, "Class-Wide Instructional Feedback: Improving Children's Academic Skill Development," in *Learning Disabilities: New Research*, ed. S. V. Randall (Hauppauge, NY: Nova Sciences, 2006), 271–85; Douglas Fisher and Nancy Frey, "Writing Instruction for Struggling Adolescent Readers: A Gradual Release Model," *Journal of Adolescent & Adult Literacy* 46, no. 5 (2002): 396–405.
7. Carol Dweck, *Mindset: The New Psychology of Success* (New York: Random House, 2006).

CHAPTER 5

1. James Rolling, *Cinderella Story: A Scholarly Sketchbook about Race, Identity, Barack Obama, the Human Spirit, and Other Stuff That Matters* (Lanham, MD: AltaMira, 2010).
2. P. David Pearson and Margaret Gallagher, "The Instruction of Reading Comprehension," *Contemporary Educational Psychology* 8 (1983): 317–44.
3. Steve Graham and Dolores Perin, *Writing Next: Effective Strategies to Improve Writing in Middle and High Schools* (New York: Carnegie Corporation, 2007).
4. Steve Graham, Charles A. MacArthur, and Jill Fitzgerald, *Best Practices in Writing Instruction* (New York: Guilford, 2013); Arthur Applebee and Judith Langer, *Writing Instruction That Works: Proven Methods for Middle and High School Classrooms* (New York: Teachers College Press, 2013).
5. Carl Nagin, *Because Writing Matters: Improving Student Writing in Our Schools* (San Francisco: Jossey-Bass, 2009); Anne Whitney, "Teacher Transformation in the National Writing Project," *Research in the Teaching of English* 43, no. 2 (2008): 144–87.
6. Kelly Gallagher, *Write Like This: Teaching Real-World Writing through Modeling and Mentor Texts* (Portsmouth, NH: Heinemann, 2011): 15.
7. See, for example, Alfred W. Tatum and Gholnecsar Muhammad, "African American Males and Literacy Development in Contexts that Are Characteristically Urban," *Urban Review* 47, no. 2 (2012): 434–63.
8. US Department of Education, *The Status of Racial Diversity in the Educator Workplace* (Washington, DC: US Department of Education, 2016).
9. This activity was adapted from the Three Words in Three Minutes activity outlined by Aimee Buckner in *Notebook Know How: Strategies for the Writer's Notebook* (Portland, ME: Stenhouse, 2005).

CHAPTER 6

1. Carl Anderson, *How's It Going? A Practical Guide to Conferring with Student Writers* (Portsmouth, NH: Heinemann, 2000); Nancie Atwell, *In the Middle: Reading, Writing and Learning with Adolescents* (Portsmouth, NH: Heinemann, 1987); Randy Bomer, *Time for Meaning* (Portsmouth, NH: Heinemann, 1995); Kelly Gallagher, *Teaching Adolescent Writers* (Portland, ME: Stenhouse: 2007); Latrise P. Johnson, "Alternative Writing Worlds: The Possibilities of Personal Writing for Adolescents," *Journal of Adolescent & Adult Literacy* 62, no. 3 (2018): 311–18; Penny Kittle, *Write Beside Them: Risk, Voice, and Clarity in High School Writing* (Portsmouth, NH: Heinemann, 2008); Linda Rief, *Read, Write, Teach: Choice and Challenge in the Reading-Writing Workshop* (Portsmouth, NH: Heinemann, 2014).
2. Cris Tovani, *So What Do They Really Know? Assessment That Informs Teaching and Learning* (Portland, ME: Stenhouse, 2011), 50.
3. Lucy Calkins, *The Art of Teaching Writing* (Portsmouth, NH: Heinemann).

4. Dylan Wiliam, *Embedded Formative Assessment* (Bloomington, IN: Solution Tree, 2011); see also Tovani, 2011.

5. Marcelle Haddix, "Black Boys Can Write: Challenging Dominant Framings of African American Adolescent Males in Literacy Research," *Journal of Adolescent and Adult Literacy* 53, no. 4 (2009): 341–43; Django Paris and Samy Alim, *Culturally Sustaining Pedagogies: Teaching and Learning for Justice in a Changing World* (New York: Teachers College Press, 2017).

6. Anderson, *How's It Going?*

7. George Hillocks, *Research on Written Composition: New Directions for Teaching* (Urbana, IL: Clearinghouse on Reading and Communication Skills, 1986).

CHAPTER 7

1. Anne Beaufort, "Writing in the Workplace," *Research on Composition: Multiple Perspectives on Two Decades of Change*, ed. Peter Smagorinsky (New York: Teachers College Press, 2006); Elke Van Steendam, "Forms of Collaboration in Writing," *Journal of Writing Research* 8, no. 2 (2016): 183–204.

2. Kelly Chandler-Olcott, "Disciplinary Literacy and Multimodal Text Design in Physical Education," *Literacy* 51, no. 3 (2017): 147–53; Jayne C. Lammers, Alicia Marie Magnifico, and Jen Scott Curwood, "Literate Identities in Fan-Based Online Affinity Spaces," *Handbook of Writing, Literacies, and Education in Digital Cultures*, ed. Kathy Mills, Amy Stornaiuolo, Anna Smith, and Jessica Pandya (New York: Routledge, 2018), 174–84.

3. Donald J. Leu Jr., J. Gregory McVerry, Ian O'Byrne, Carita Kilili, Lisa Zawilinski, Heidi Everett-Cacopardo, Clint Kennedy, and Elena Forzani, "The New Literacies of Online Reading Comprehension: Expanding the Literacy and Learning Curriculum," *Journal of Adolescent & Adult Literacy* 55, no. 1 (2011): 5–14.

4. Judith Langer, "Beating the Odds: Teaching Middle and High School Students to Read and Write Well," *American Educational Research Journal* 38, no. 4 (2001): 837–80.

5. Steve Graham and Dolores Perin, *Writing Next: Effective Strategies to Improve Writing in Middle and High Schools* (New York: Carnegie Corporation, 2007).

6. Steve Graham, Charles A. MacArthur, and Jill Fitzgerald, *Best Practices in Writing Instruction* (New York: Guilford, 2013); Amy Wilson-Lopez and Angela Minichiello, "Disciplinary Literacy in Engineering," *Journal of Adolescent & Adult Literacy* 61, no. 1 (2017): 7–14.

7. Kelly Chandler-Olcott and Paula Kluth, "'Mother's Voice Was the Main Source of Learning': Parents' Role in Supporting the Literacy Development of Students with Autism," *Journal of Literacy Research* 40, no. 4 (2009): 461–92; Kelly Chandler-Olcott and Paula Kluth, "Why Everyone Benefits from Including Students with Autism in Literacy Classrooms," *Reading Teacher* 62, no. 7 (2009): 548–57; Paula Kluth and Kelly Chandler-Olcott, *A Land We Can Share: Teaching Literacy to Students with Autism* (Baltimore: Paul Brookes, 2008).

8. James Britton, *Language and Learning* (Coral Gables, FL: University of Miami Press, 1970).

9. James Flood, Diane Lapp, Sharon Flood, and Greta Nagel, "'Am I Allowed to Group?' Using Flexible Patterns for Effective Instruction," *Reading Teacher* 45, no. 8 (1992): 608–616.

10. For more on the evolution in our thinking, see Kelly Chandler-Olcott and Janine Nieroda, "The Evolution and Creation of a Co-Teaching Community: How Teachers Learned to Address Adolescent English Language Learners' Needs as Writers," *Equity and Excellence in Education* 49, no. 2 (2016): 170–82.

11. Kelly Gallagher, *Teaching Adolescent Writers* (Portland, ME: Stenhouse, 2006).

12. The clip has since been removed from the internet at the request of Thomas's label, but other "making of" videos that might be used in similar ways are widely available on YouTube and other video streaming services.

CHAPTER 8

1. H. Richard Milner, IV, "Beyond a Test Score: Explaining Opportunity Gaps in Educational Practice," *Journal of Black Studies* 43, no. 6 (2012): 693–718.

2. George Hillocks, *The Testing Trap: How State Assessments Control Learning* (New York: Teachers College Press, 2002); Judith Langer, "Beating the Odds: Teaching Middle and High School Students to Read and Write Well," *American Educational Research Journal* 38, no. 4 (2001): 837–80; Sarah McCarthey, "The Impact of No Child Left Behind on Teachers' Writing Instruction," *Written Communication* 25, no. 4 (2008): 464–505.

3. On school reform initiatives in the US, see, for example, Heather Zavadsky, *Bringing School Reform to Scale: Five Award-Winning Urban Districts* (Cambridge, MA: Harvard Education Press, 2009). On comparative analyses of other countries, see Linda Darling-Hammond, Dion Burns, Carol Campbell, A. Lin Goodwin, Karen Hammerness, Ee-Ling Low, Ann McIntyre, Mistilina Sato, and Kenneth Zeichner, *Empowered Educators: High-Performing Systems Shape Teaching Quality around the World* (San Francisco: Jossey-Bass, 2017); Marc Tucker, *Surpassing Shanghai: An Agenda for American Education Built on the World's Leading Systems* (Cambridge, MA: Harvard Education Press, 2011).

4. Clea Fernandez and Makoto Yoshida, *Lesson Study: A Japanese Approach to Improving Teaching and Learning* (New York: Routledge, 2004); Catherine C. Lewis and Jacqueline Hurd, *Lesson Study Step by Step: How Teaching Learning Communities Improve Instruction* (Portsmouth, NH: Heinemann, 2011).

5. Linda Christensen, *Reading, Writing, and Rising Up: Teaching about Social Justice and the Power of the Written Word* (Milwaukee: Rethinking Schools, 2017); Steve Graham, Charles A. MacArthur, and Jill Fitzgerald, *Best Practices in Writing Instruction* (New York: Guilford, 2013).

6. Several of my Syracuse colleagues have conducted collaborative research with teachers and school leaders establishing a link between school restructuring to promote inclusion, increased achievement, and an increased sense of belonging for students; for more, see Julie Causton-Theoharis, George Theoharis, Thomas Bull, Meghan Cosier, and Kathy Dempf-Aldrich, "Schools of Promise:

A School District-University Partnership Centered on School Reform," *Remedial and Special Education* 32, no. 3 (2011): 192–205.

7. During this period the Brown district adopted and implemented Talent Development's Strategic Reading program (http://www.tdschools.org/about /curriculum-instruction/language-arts/strategic-reading) across the district for ninth graders who are seen as needing support with comprehension and fluency.

8. Bryan Ripley Crandall, "Writing with Ubuntu in Support of Refugee and Immigrant Youth," *English in Texas* 46, no. 2 (2016): 12–17.

9. Pamela Grossman, Karen Hammerness, and Morva McDonald, "Redefining Teaching, Reimagining Teacher Education," *Teachers and Teaching: Theory and Practice* 15, no. 2 (2009): 273–89; Lee Shulman, "Theory, Practice, and the Education of Professionals," *Elementary School Journal* 98, no. 5 (1998): 511–26; Kenneth Zeichner, "The Turn Once Again toward Practice-Based Teacher Education," *Journal of Teacher Education* 63, no. 5 (2013): 376–82.

10. Kristien Zenkov and Kristine Pytash, *Clinical Experiences in Teacher Education: Critical, Project-Based Interventions in Diverse Classrooms* (New York: Routledge, 2018), 2.

11. Kelly Chandler-Olcott, Sharon Dotger, Heather Waymouth, Michael Crosby, Molly Lahr, Kathleen Hinchman, Keith Newvine, and Janine Nieroda, "Teacher Candidates Learn to Enact Curriculum in a Partnership-Sponsored Literacy Enrichment Program for Youth," *New Educator* 14, no. 3 (2018): 192–211; Kelly Chandler-Olcott, Sharon Dotger, Heather Waymouth, Keith Newvine, and Kathleen Hinchman, "Learning to Teach Literacy through Lesson Study in a University-School Partnership," paper presented at the Annual Meeting of the Literacy Research Association, Tampa, Florida, December 2017.

12. Richard Allington and Anne McGill-Franzen, *Summer Reading: Closing the Rich/Poor Reading Achievement Gap* (New York: Teachers College Press, 2013); Sarah Pitcock, "The Case for Summer Learning: Why Supporting Students and Families All Year Is Vitally Important," *American Educator* (Spring 2018): 4–8.

13. See, for example, Zenkov and Pytash, *Clinical Experiences*; and Monica Ferguson, Janice Dole, Laura Scarpulla, and Sharon Adamson, "A Summer Program to Assist Diverse, Urban Adolescents in Becoming College and Career Ready," *Journal of Adolescent & Adult Literacy* 62, no. 1 (2018): 79–87.

14. Jayne C. Lammers, "What Happens When Fanfiction Goes to School? The Challenges and Opportunities of Teacher-Supported Network Writing," paper presented at the Annual Meeting of the Literacy Research Association, Nashville, Tennessee, December 2016.

15. For more on the potentially negative effects of tracking, see Jeannie Oakes, *Keeping Track: How Schools Structure Inequality* (New Haven, CT: Yale University Press, 2005); and Eric Hanushek and Ludger Woessman, "Does Educational Tracking Affect Performance and Inequality?," *Economic Journal* 116, no. 510 (2006): C63–C76.

Acknowledgments

Because this project was both collaborative and longitudinal, I have a long list of people to thank:

- Mark Austin, Jenniffer Benedetto, Jodi Burnash, Anne Daviau, Maureen DeChick, Danielle Donahue, Michele Gendron, Ellie Leach, Heather Moses, Maureen Kendrick Page, Jimmy Smith, Jolene Todd, John Zeleznik, and Sara Zizzi are consummate professionals who put kids first. It was a privilege to learn from and with each of you.
- For leadership and optimism about the potential of urban schools, I am grateful to Ella Briand, Sharon Contreras, Donna Formica, Daniel Lowengard, Debbie Mastropaolo, David Maynard, and Rhonda Zajac.
- Cedric Bolton, Katharine Chang, Donna Ditota, Elise Ginkel, Maureen Green, Tula Goenka, Katelyn Kanavy, Nader Maroun, Neal Powless, Crystal Rhode, James Rolling, Robert Wilson, and especially Bud Poliquin generously agreed to share insights from their personal and professional lives when they served as guest writers.
- Douglas Biklen, Jeffery Mangram, Christy Ashby, and the inimitable Mary Taylor offered staunch, long-term support for the early college initiative in general and the writing institute in particular.
- Both the institute and I benefited from the insights and contributions of Syracuse University graduate students Lorraine Adu-Krow, Bryan Crandall, Paul Czuprynski, Bridget Lawson, Janine Nieroda, Carrie Rood, and Lauren Shallish.
- Twenty years after joining the department, I continue to be sustained and inspired by my Reading and Language Arts colleagues in Syracuse University's School of Education, including Rachel Brown, Kathleen Hinchman, Bong Gee Jang, Zaline Roy-Campbell, Louise Wilkinson, and, especially, our fierce and fearless chair, Marcelle Haddix.

- Sharon Dotger, Kathleen Hinchman, and David Reinking problem solved and commiserated with me about the challenges of conducting design-based research in education. Each offered advice and feedback that kept me from giving up on this project on more than one occasion.
- It was a genuine pleasure to work with Nancy Walser, whose suggestions for improving the manuscript were always smart and supportive.
- I owe a huge debt to my mother, Gail Gibson, for being my first and best writing teacher, for helping to shape these ideas through near daily phone calls over more than a decade, and for reading every word of this manuscript in draft form.
- Jim, Lucy, and Quinn Olcott gave me space to write when I needed it and plenty of wonderful reasons to stop when it was time.

About the Author

KELLY CHANDLER-OLCOTT is Laura J. and L. Douglas Meredith Professor for Teaching Excellence in the Syracuse University School of Education, where she coordinates undergraduate and graduate programs in English education. Her scholarly interests include design-based research, literacy across the disciplines, and collaborative approaches to teacher education in diverse, inclusive settings. The author of five other books and more than seventy-five chapters and articles, she is currently serving a six-year term as coeditor with Dr. Kathleen A. Hinchman of the International Literacy Association's *Journal of Adolescent & Adult Literacy*.

Index